The Secret Files of Kara Danvers

My name is Kara Zor-El.

But that's not the name most people recognize. To my family and friends I'm Kara Danvers, a reporter for CatCo Worldwide Media in National City. To the rest of the world, I'm known only as Supergirl. The book you hold in your hands is my personal account of my life as a superhero. It's a scrapbook of sorts—a way for me to see how far I've come from the scared little girl rocketed to Earth from her dying planet, Krypton. If you're reading this, I'm trusting you with my most valued secrets, my most important memories. I have a responsibility to this city and to the people I care about. And now, you also share in that responsibility.

Like my cousin, Superman, in Metropolis, I strive to be a symbol of hope to a world that desperately needs it. And while there will always be those who fear what they don't understand, I'd like to think I'm helping to make this world a better place, if only a little at a time.

My name is Kara Zor-El. Kara Danvers. Supergirl. Welcome to my world.

Nothing quite like going through old family photos.

True, most people don't have to rely on grainy files that traveled with them for light-years from a dying planet, but I'll take what I can get. I was born on the planet Krypton, in a solar system revolving around a red sun. I remember a lot about my childhood, even if I don't have many pictures to prove it. Krypton was home, and it will always be a part of me.

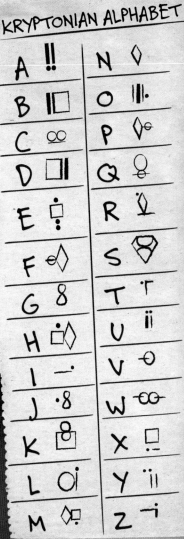

KRYPTONIAN ALPHABET

A	‼	N	◊
B	▯□	O	⫴.
C	∞	P	◊̸
D	□▮	Q	♀
E	⬚̈	R	◊̧
F	◇⬦	S	⬡
G	8	T	⌐
H	□◇	U	⁓̈
I	—·	V	⊖
J	·8	W	∞
K	⬚̺	X	□⁚
L	◯̇	Y	⁚
M	◇̺	Z	⁓⁀

Alura

I remember my mother, Alura, very clearly. The smell of her hair. The little looks she'd give me across the dinner table when Dad was telling one of his drawn-out stories. I always wanted to be just like her. I guess I still do.

Astra

My mother had a twin sister named Astra. Back on Krypton, I considered her the "fun aunt." I can't even begin to count how many nights we spent outside, looking up at the stars. She was a different person when I met her again years later.

Dad

Zor-El. The backbone of our family. Mom held all the political power, but Dad held us together. I miss him every day.

Little baby Kal-El

I hardly got to know him before . . . before it all came tumbling down.

The rocket ship.

Thirty-five years ago, Krypton teetered on the verge of destruction. My aunt Lara and uncle Jor-El, decided to send their son, Kal-El, to Earth in a rocket ship to save his life. My parents did the same for me.

I was meant to protect my cousin, to keep him safe when we landed on our strange new world called Earth. It was my only mission.

But I never got the chance to see it through.

ITEM

SUPERGIRL'S ROCKET SHIP

My mother gave me this necklace as something to remember her by. Years later, I gave it to someone special to me. Few things remind me more of home.

In a heartbeat, everything I ever knew was gone. But while Kal-El's rocket proceeded to Earth as planned, Krypton's destruction sent out a shock wave that knocked my own ship off course.

Drastically off course.

My rocket ship was sent spiraling into a timeless region of space known as the Phantom Zone. I slept there unchanged while time passed without me. After twenty-four years, my rocket mysteriously dislodged, and my ship was able to correct course and follow its programming.

And I finally came to Earth.

I later discovered that I wasn't alone during my time in the Phantom Zone. In her role as a judicator, my mother had used the anomaly of the Phantom Zone as a place to cage violent prisoners. The worst criminals that Krypton had to offer—alongside offenders from other worlds,—were imprisoned in a place called Fort Rozz. There they waited out their sentences.

But what I didn't know then was that when I escaped the Phantom Zone, so did they.

Kal-El had twenty-four years on Earth without me. Thanks to the yellow sun's radiation beating down on Earth, he had become by far the strongest man on the planet. The world called him Superman, but in secret—when he wasn't wearing his red cape and the symbol of the House of El on his chest—he lived as a newspaper reporter named Clark Kent.

Clark didn't need my protection, but he knew I needed his. To keep me safe and out of the public eye, he arranged for Eliza and Jeremiah Danvers to take me in. While they already had their hands full with their own daughter, Alex, they accepted me as one of their own, and helped me hide my powers as a normal teenage girl named Kara Danvers.

Dear Diary,

Sorry if my English isn't too great yet. I didn't have much time to study it back on Krypton. It's one thing to memorize this weird alphabet. It's another to actually get my hand to form these letters. I miss Kryptonese.

I miss a lot of things.

Eliza and Jeremiah are taking good care of me. They probably know more about Kryptonians than anyone else on this planet besides Kal. And Eliza's really trying to include me in everything. I'm just not up for it yet. I already have a family. Not sure I need this new one. Especially Alex.

I don't know what her deal is, but she acts like I'm intentionally trying to ruin her life. She has everything she could ever want. A mom, a dad, a great house, friends at school. I think she's jealous of what I can do. Wonder if she would still be if she knew I'd trade my powers in a heartbeat to be with my family again, even for just an hour.

Anyway, gotta go. Eliza's making something called meat loaf for dinner tonight. Apparently it's an Earth delicacy. I should at least try it, I guess.

Kara

Jeremiah Danvers

Jeremiah Danvers. My foster father. He convinced me that the world already had a Superman and that I was at my best when I was just being myself. He was the one who gave me my first pair of glasses, which became part of Kara Danvers's signature look. I didn't need them to see, but the lead they were lined with certainly kept my vision powers in check.

Jeremiah disappeared almost fifteen years ago. I didn't find out why until recently.

Eliza Danvers

She can be as stubborn as the women she raised, but Eliza Danvers is also one of the most loving people I've ever met. From the very start, she didn't try to replace my mom, but she let me know that I mattered. She let me know that when I was Kara Danvers, I was safe.

Those are powerful words to a girl who'd just lost her world.

Alex Danvers

Alex. The sister I never wanted but now can't live without. It took us a while to find common ground, but once we did, we couldn't believe how much of it there was. She's my best friend and has become the most important person in my life.

Home

Our little piece of heaven in Midvale. Still the best place I know to go when I need to clear my head.

Streaky

Don't ask how he got that name. You don't want to know.

Midvale was a great place to grow up, but like Clark, I wanted to be where the action was. Instead of Metropolis, I thought I'd find a town of my own where I could make my mark.

So I packed up and headed to National City.

Guide To:
NATIONAL CITY

All the sights and sounds of this beautiful western Metropolis.

NC
Tourism

Midtown Park

Simmons
Square

CATCO ➡
Worldwide

Well, that was one way to make an impression . . .

Just finished my interview at CatCo Worldwide Media, and I would be very surprised if I ever set foot in that building again. A nice guy—I think his name was Winn? Winnie?—sort of hinted to me on my way in that Ms. Grant goes through assistants like water. If he was warning me, I guess I should have listened.

Either way, she's a piece of work. Rude. Holier than thou. But very driven. Working for her would be a huge sacrifice, but I get the feeling that she sacrifices just as much. Geez. Look at me rationalizing the way Ms. Grant talks down to people. I guess I did want this job more than I thought. I just want a place to really belong. To really make a difference to someone, someone important.

Hold that thought. Phone's ringing.

Well, that was certainly unexpected. Looks like I'll be seeing a lot more of Ms. Grant. Kara Danvers, personal assistant to Cat Grant, the CEO of a worldwide media conglomerate.

Guess I made a better first impression than I thought.

Kara

Cat Grant. CEO. Mentor. The toughest boss a Girl of Steel could ask for.

CATCO WORLDWIDE MEDIA

KARA DANVERS
PERSONAL ASSISTANT TO CAT GRANT

EMPLOYEE ID #: ACT252

CO WORLDWIDE MEDIA

THE CAT WHO DEVOURED THE CANARY

By Jerry Wolfman

Meeting Cat Grant is like entering a boxing ring where the world heavyweight champ is waiting for you, knocking his gloves together. You have to have your arms up, your vitals covered, and be ready to go on the offensive if you hope to get any decent jabs in. Even then, you're probably destined to be hit with a KO in the first round.

As the owner and CEO of CatCo Worldwide Media, Cat Grant is undoubtedly the most powerful woman in National City. That fact hasn't gone unnoticed by Ms. Grant. Despite her rather modest roots peddling Metropolis gossip in the often-overlooked society pages of the *Daily Planet,* Cat is no longer worried about what the public thinks. She is headstrong, determined, and quite possibly the most terrifying person I've ever sat down with for an interview.

The product of an overbearing mother and an unrelenting desire to make something of herself, Ms. Grant moved to National City from Metropolis, first acquiring the *National City Tribune* on her path to becoming a media mogul.

SUPERMAN
In Pictures

The Photography of James Olsen

James's Pulitzer Prize–winning image. The first photograph of Superman.

Apparently Clark posed for this. Um, cheat much?

AN EXHIBIT AT THE SIEGEL AND SHUSTER GALLERY

James Olsen wasn't at all what I was expecting. When I first heard he was transferring to CatCo, I expected him to look like his reputation. People knew him not just as the first person to ever photograph the Man of Steel, but also as "Superman's Pal." I figured he would be some scrawny kid with red hair and freckles or something.

I couldn't have been more wrong. Not to sound superficial, but the James Olsen I met would put every lead actor in a soap opera to shame. There was an instant spark between us. Or at least, I hoped there was . . .

What I didn't know when I first met James was that he wasn't just in National City to start a new life. He was also there as a favor to my cousin, to look out for me. Superman had given James this signal watch years ago, one that emits a frequency so high-pitched that only the Man of Steel can detect it.

Well, I can hear it, too. But I don't like to brag.

And then this happened.

NATIONAL CITY

TRIBUNE

VOL. 134 - No. 15/Sun and Clouds, 70°/ Weather P.14   WEEKDAY EDITION © CATCO   DESIGNATED AREAS HIGHER   Price $1.00

FLYING WOMAN PREVENTS PLANE DISASTER

Does National City Have Its Own Superhero?

I didn't have much choice. Alex was on Flight 237 when its engine failed over National City. It was time for me to stop pretending to be normal. It was time to show the world who I really was.

No matter the consequences.

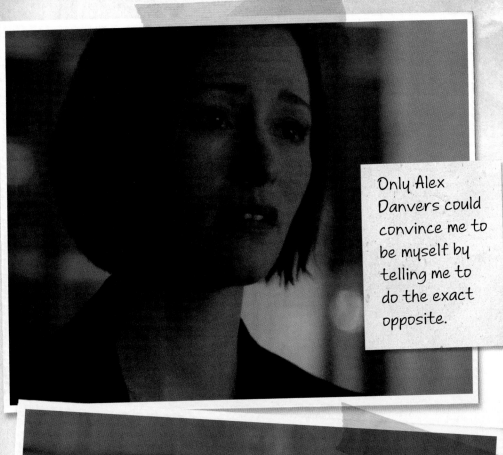

Only Alex Danvers could convince me to be myself by telling me to do the exact opposite.

Another of the survivors of Flight 237, Thomas Coville.

In an offhand comment at CatCo, my coworker and friend Winslow Schott Jr. mentioned that the world would never take the hero of Flight 237 seriously until she wore her own supersuit, like Superman. I dismissed the idea at first, but when I realized I'd need allies in my new life as a hero, Winn was the first person I turned to.

Surprisingly enough, Winn has a background in design. He came up with plenty of concepts for my supersuit, some of which would have been better off staying in his imagination . . .

This is not something I'd even wear to the beach, Winn! Try again!

I DON'T CARE WHAT YOU SAY, KARA. CAPES ARE SO 1970. LEAVE IT THIS WAY.

Winn! Cape! Now!!

The cape helps with aerodynamics. Although something bulletproof would be a big plus . . .

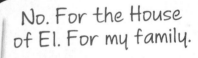

CAPE'S MADE FROM A STRUCTURED POLYMER COMPOSITE. THAT SHOULD WORK FOR YOU.

PLUS, THIS ONE HAS THE S FOR "SUPER," LIKE YOUR COUSIN.

No. For the House of El. For my family.

YEAH, BUT ALSO FOR "SUPER." BECAUSE YOU LIVE ON EARTH NOW. AND WE'VE BEEN OVER THIS, BUT NO ONE KNOWS KRYPTONIAN HERE!!!

As it turned out, Winn won that particular argument. Because within a day, Cat Grant had named me "Supergirl."

Winn Schott Jr. My best friend at CatCo, despite his sense of fashion . . . and humor.

No sooner had I started to get my act together as a superhero then I was shot and drugged by the secret government organization called the Department of Extranormal Operations.

When I woke up in their secure facility, I realized that the DEO wasn't just a military branch concerned about National City's new so-called "alien threat." It was the secret employer of my sister, Alex.

The Department of Extranormal Operations

Notes: The Earth's first line of defense against alien invasions of any scale, the DEO was formed after Supergirl's rocket ship crash-landed on Earth, bringing with it Fort Rozz, the Kryptonian prison formerly located in the Phantom Zone. With the Earth overrun by the worst beings in the galaxy, the formation of the DEO became a necessity.

ALIAS
Kara Zor-El, Kara Danvers

POWERS/ABILITIES
Super-strength, endurance, speed, agility, and durability; heat, microscopic, x-ray, and telescopic vision; accelerated healing; freeze breath; flight

HOMEWORLD
Krypton

WEAKNESSES
Kryptonite, red sun radiation, magic manipulation

SUPERGIRL

So I decided that to best serve my city as Supergirl, I needed to work through the DEO as one of their agents. While I wasn't sure I was much of a team player at first, at least I was in good company.

ALIAS
No known alias

POWERS/ABILITIES
Expert markswoman; trained in hand-to-hand combat; proficient in martial arts, espionage, and survival techniques; trained in a variety of human and alien weapons; expert medical knowledge; proficient with hi-tech devices and computers

HOMEWORLD
Earth

WEAKNESSES
Has shown loyalty to friends and family over DEO on occasion; human susceptible to conventional attacks

ALEX DANVERS

ALIAS
No known alias

POWERS/ABILITIES
Expertly trained soldier; precise markswoman; connections to high-ranking government officials, including General Sam Lane

HOMEWORLD
Earth

WEAKNESSES
Seems to jump around from career to career with little job loyalty; susceptible to conventional attacks

LUCY LANE

ALIAS
No known alias

POWERS/ABILITIES
Genius-level intellect with a background in various sciences including astronomy; adopted father of Kara Zor-El (SEE: Supergirl); computer expert proven to possess remarkable hacking skills; highly trained soldier with weapons expertise; trained in hand-to-hand combat; possesses cybernetic body parts that enhance strength, endurance, and durability

HOMEWORLD
Earth

WEAKNESSES
Strong personal convictions have caused him to clash with orders on occasion

JEREMIAH DANVERS

MARTIAN MANHUNTER

ALIAS
J'onn J'onzz, Hank
Henshaw

POWERS/ABILITIES
Psychic abilities, including
telepathy; shapeshifting;
invisibility; intangibility; flight;
superstrength; enhanced
durability, endurance, and
agility; knowledge of alien
cultures; highly trained soldier
and marksman; expert hand-to-
hand combatant; knowledge of
Martian fighting techniques

HOMEWORLD
Mars

WEAKNESSES
Fire

Like everyone working at the DEO, I originally took Director Hank Henshaw at face value. What I didn't know at the time was that he wasn't Henshaw at all. The real Henshaw disappeared while trying to execute a peaceful Martian named J'onn J'onzz. My father, Jeremiah Danvers, tried to stop Henshaw and was seemingly killed in the process.

After swearing to my father to keep my family safe, J'onn shapeshifted into Henshaw's form and became the director of the DEO. Although an alien himself, J'onn did a better job of protecting Earth from alien threats than Hank ever did.

Some might call that ironic, but as an alien myself, it just sounds like par for the course.

Fort Rozz

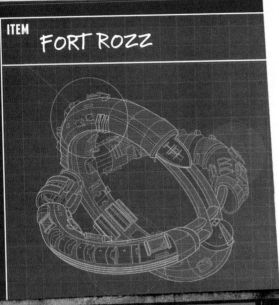

ITEM
FORT ROZZ

Krypton's maximum-security prison. Most of its inmates were sentenced there by my mother, Alura, to help keep Krypton safe. So it goes without saying that when the Fort was dragged out of the Phantom Zone, I wasn't exactly a favorite of any of the escapees.

VARTOX

ALIAS
No known alias

POWERS/ABILITIES
Superstrength that allows leaping over great distances; enhanced durability, speed, agility, and endurance; utilizes atomic axe that can pierce even Kryptonian skin

HOMEWORLD
Valeron

WEAKNESSES
Atomic axe will explode at superhot temperatures

Vartox stabbed himself in the chest after I was finally able to defeat him on one of my first missions. He died telling me about a threat to come. Yeah, that's not ominous at all . . .

ALIAS
No known alias

POWERS/ABILITIES
Superstrength that allows leaping over great distances; shapeshifting; lethal stingers; enhanced senses, including smell; other insectoid qualities

HOMEWORLD
Hellgram

WEAKNESSES
Vulnerable to his own stingers

HELLGRAMMITE

An unnamed alien of the Hellgrammite race. I was able to identify the shapeshifter from research I did as a girl back on Krypton. As Alex later found out, Hellgrammite stingers are poisonous, even to themselves.

ALIAS
No known alias

POWERS/ABILITIES
Psychic powers, including telepathy and mind control; superstrength, endurance, and durability; extensive history of defeating other alien races, including the vaunted Faceless Hunters; able to shoot energy blasts from the gem in his forehead

HOMEWORLD
Saturn

WEAKNESSES
Able to be contained using neural shielding or inhibitors

JEMM

Jemm escaped his cell at the DEO when an earthquake temporarily knocked out the base's power. Luckily, Alex and J'onn were there to take him down.

ASTRA

Twins were rare on Krypton, but my mother, Alura, and her twin, Astra, were alike in appearance only. I loved and adored Astra, but she chose to walk a dark path while my mother chose the light, even going so far as to imprison her own twin on Fort Rozz.

NON

Astra's lieutenant and husband, Non, was completely faithful to my aunt. It seems so strange that a man capable of such love could be so blinded by his hatred for Earthlings.

ALIAS

No known alias

POWERS/ABILITIES

Superstrength, endurance, durability, and agility; many connections in the criminal underworld

HOMEWORLD

Unknown

WEAKNESSES

Can be overwhelmed by large armed forces

MANDRAX

Not all of the escaped inmates from Fort Rozz were up to Earth-shattering plots. Mandrax decided to become the head of an alien art smuggling ring, which the DEO was later able to bring to justice.

Way more excited than he should've been about my superhero career, Winn took it upon himself to convert the office of someone named Ed Flaherty at CatCo into Supergirl's own secret headquarters, right in the heart of National City.

CATCO
MAGAZINE

SUPERGIRL
TAKES ON THE
WORLD
WHO IS SHE?
THE NEW GIRL
IN TOWN
IS FLYING HIGH

FIND YOUR
BALANCE
MAKE YOUR
INVESTMENTS
WORK FOR YOU

LADIES IN
POWER:
50 WOMEN
WHO WON'T
BACK DOWN
SHATTERING
THE GLASS
CEILING

ALL THE HOT SPOTS
THE FUN GIRLS' GUIDE
TO NATIONAL CITY

MY CONVERSATION WITH
SUPERGIRL

By Cat Grant

If anything, she certainly shares Superman's flair for the dramatic.

When Supergirl agreed to meet with me, she did so in true superheroic fashion. Throwing caution to the wind and risking a rather hefty lawsuit, she lifted my sedan and flew me to the top of a skyscraper. She wanted my attention, and I'll be honest: it worked.

While she seemed a bit nervous for our one on one, perhaps uneasy with speaking to human beings of any stature, she nevertheless let me record our conversation. I'll admit, our talk was certainly more revealing than I was expecting.

Cat Grant: Okay, Supergirl. Let's start with the generals. Where are you from?

Supergirl: I traveled to Earth from my home planet.

CG: Krypton.

SG: Yes. When it was destroyed. My parents sent me here, where they thought I'd be safe.

CG: I feel like I've heard this story before.

SG: This is my story.

CG: So I can assume that all of your powers are the same as the Man of Steel's? The flying, the superstrength, the freezey-breath thing?

SG: I'm still working on that last one.

CG: Oh. So you're not up to his level yet.

At this point in the conversation, I had to dodge a blast of heat vision. Apparently, Supergirl's skin is thick enough to deflect bullets, just not criticism.

SG: I wouldn't say that.

CG: So why are we just hearing from you now?

SG: I'm not sure I understand the question.

CG: Well, if you've been on Earth for years, why wait this long to start giving back? Where were you during the earthquake two years ago or the wildfires last September that killed eight people?

SG: This is not a job I take lightly. I had to be ready.

CG: Any plans to start a family?

SG: Nobody ever asks my cousin these questions.

CG: Superman is your cousin?

SG: This interview is over.

As she flew off in a super-huff, I was left with more questions than answers. But despite her camera-shy attitude, I was able to learn one thing at least. The S seems to run in the family.
CONTINUED ON PAGE 28.

CONTINUED ON PAGE 28.

ALIAS
Ben Krull

POWERS/ABILITIES
Fires highly concentrated bursts of nuclear energy from his gauntlets; armored chest plate provides increased strength and flight

HOMEWORLD
Earth

WEAKNESSES
Can be tracked by radiation signature; suit runs on a plutonium core that will shut him down if removed

DAILY PLANET

DAILY PLANET

★ ★ ★ ★   DAILY PLANET

Thursday, August 9, 2018 $1.50

SUPERMAN VS. REACTRON!
WITH METROPOLIS IN THE BALANCE

By Lois Lane

METROPOLIS – It was like something out of a 1980s disaster film. Buildings burned. Panicked civilians ran for cover. Storm clouds thundered above as two titans clashed on what used to resemble 5th Avenue. One figure, in his red cape and blue suit, was instantly familiar to the men and women of Metropolis. The other, in glowing armor smoldering from battle, was not. Over the din of the crowd, car alarms, and gas explosions, we all heard his name shouted in a fit of rage: "Reactron." STORY CONTINUED ON 2B.

Ben Krull became Reactron after he and his wife were caught in an explosion at Bakerline Nuclear Power Station, near Metropolis. While Superman stopped the plant from a full-on meltdown, Krull blamed the Man of Steel for the death of his wife, who didn't survive the event.

As Reactron, Krull fought Superman numerous times. When he found out I was Superman's cousin, I became guilty by association. With the help of the DEO, I was able to finally beat him by removing his power source.

I stopped Reactron. Something even Superman never did. I don't think I stopped smiling for a week.

ALIVE AND WIRED WITH
LESLIE ★ WILLIS

STRAIGHT FROM CATCO PLAZA
TALK SO GOOD, IT'S SHOCKING!

Leslie Willis wasn't a fan of Supergirl. In fact, she took every opportunity to trash me on her radio show. She hurt the "brand" that Cat Grant was so desperately trying to cultivate, so in response, Cat banished Leslie to the traffic beat. A twist of fate and a stray bolt of lightning turned Leslie Willis into Livewire, an electrically powered metahuman.

ALIAS
Leslie Willis

POWERS/ABILITIES
Controls and manipulates electrical energy; able to travel through electric wires and cords by transforming to pure electricity

HOMEWORLD
Earth

WEAKNESSES
Water; nonconductive materials; vulnerable in human form

LIVEWIRE

ALIAS
No known alias

POWERS/ABILITIES
Genius-level intellect; has a multibillion-dollar company at his disposal; possesses nearly unlimited access to hi-tech weaponry and other genius scientific minds

HOMEWORLD
Earth

WEAKNESSES
His arrogance makes him vulnerable to attacks he deems impossible

MAXWELL LORD

Who commissions a giant portrait of himself for his office wall? Maxwell Lord, that's who.

He's one of the richest men in National City, and the CEO of Lord Technologies. I instantly knew there was something untrustworthy about Lord. That doesn't mean I was happy to find out that my suspicions were correct.

IT'S A BIRD, IT'S A TRAIN!

BY SARA KARLIN

Lord Technologies has always been a trailblazer in the field of engineering. Tomorrow, the company, run by founder and CEO Maxwell Lord, is planning the maiden voyage for its Super Rail, a fitting name for a railway in National City, the home of the hero known as Supergirl.

Boasting that his train can reach speeds of up to 500 kilometers per hour, Lord had this to say about the rail's maiden voyage: "We anticipate a smooth launch." Lord continued, "National City doesn't need an alien to inspire its people. True ingenuity has always been a human trait."

The Super Rail is scheduled to take its first high-speed passenger trip tomorrow evening at eight o'clock.

Not only did Lord schedule his Super Rail's launch, but he also arranged for a man to bomb it. A man lost his life, and countless more could have died, if I hadn't intervened.

But that was Lord's plan all along. It was all a test to measure my limits. A sick game orchestrated by a very sick mind.

ALIAS
No known alias

POWERS/ABILITIES
Android usually controlled remotely by inventor T. O. Morrow; super-strength, endurance, and durability; able to fly and manipulate wind currents, from a slight breeze to a powerful weaponized tornado

HOMEWORLD
Earth

WEAKNESSES
Originally could be stopped by removing its controller, but when the robot went AWOL, it proved susceptible to intense and unrelenting heat vision attack

RED TORNADO

ITEM RED TORNADO ANDROID – PROTOTYPE
SCHEMATIC BY T.O. MORROW

NEURAL GUIDANCE FUNCTIONS

ENHANCED SENSORY RELAY

RECHARGEABLE HYBRID BATTERY CELL

STABILIZING PROPULSION SYSTEM

WAIST ROTATION FOR ENHANCED FLIGHT AND SPEED

MINIATURE ROCKET LAUNCHER HOUSED IN EACH ARM

ROTATION CAPABLE OF 350 MPH WIND PROJECTION

REINFORCED JOINTS AND EXTERIOR TO RESIST IMPACT AND GUNFIRE

ALIAS
No known alias

POWERS/ABILITIES
Strategic expert; has advanced military and hand-to-hand combat training; has powerful connections in politics and government

HOMEWORLD
Earth

WEAKNESSES
Human susceptible to conventional attacks; has soft spot for daughters Lois and Lucy Lane

GENERAL SAM LANE

While he believes he is on the side of the angels, General Lane is no fan of Kryptonians. Maybe it has something to do with his daughter, Lois, being so friendly with Metropolis's Man of Steel.

Either way, he has purposely stood in the way of the DEO (and me) several times now, even using his daughter, Lucy, to further his goals.

Dear Diary,

It's been two days. Forty-eight hours of pain, aches, and something I'm told is called a "stress headache." Ugh. Being human is the worst.

Okay, so I'm still not exactly human, but I might as well be. All my life, I wanted to be normal and fit in, and then when it happens—when I lose my powers because I used up too much solar energy fighting the Red Tornado—I can't think of anything else but getting my powers back.

The Kryptonian simulation of my mother back at the DEO assures me that my powers will come back anytime now. Alex says the same thing. But all that talk means squat when I'm stuck on the bus, sitting by a ten-year-old with a cold. How do people do this every day? And why don't I own a single pair of comfortable shoes?

Now if you'll excuse me, I have to go and clean out the closest drugstore's tissue selection. And then I think I'll take a nap.

For like
nine years.

Of course National City would choose a day when I had no powers to have one of its worst earthquakes on record. Luckily, when James fell down an elevator shaft at CatCo, my adrenaline spiked, which made my powers return.

That's James Olsen for you. Always pushing me in the right direction, even when he doesn't mean to.

Supergirl's Secret Identity:
What we know so far . . .

- *Kara takes it personally when I first name Supergirl. Why does the name mean so much to her?*

- *She flees the scene during the Livewire attack on CatCo. A few seconds later, Supergirl shows up.*

- *Kara gets sick for the first time since I've known her right during the National City earthquake. An earthquake where Supergirl is noticeably missing.*

- *She overhears Dirk after a board meeting. I'm standing next to her and hear nothing. Do my ears need to be checked, or is Kara's hearing remarkable? Dare I say . . . super?*

- *They look remarkably alike, once one gets over Kara's rather frumpy demeanor. Is my personal assistant the most powerful woman in National City? (Present company excluded, of course.)*

One thing I will say about working at the DEO: it's very helpful when your supervisor just happens to be a shapeshifting Martian.

The only way I was able to throw Cat Grant off my trail was when J'onn took Supergirl's form, allowing "Supergirl" and me to both visit Ms. Grant at the same time.

ALIAS
Winslow Schott Sr.

POWERS/ABILITIES
Genius-level intellect with a
bizarre obsession with weap-
onizing toys; engineering and
computer expert

HOMEWORLD
Earth

WEAKNESSES
Human susceptible to conventional attacks

DEO

TOYMAN

When the Toyman attempted to involve his son, Winn Schott Jr., in a plot for revenge on National City, my cousin sent over an old prison interview he'd conducted with the Toyman some time after Schott was first jailed.

Clark Kent: Hello, Mr. Schott. Thanks for sitting down with me today.

Winslow Schott: I prefer "Toyman" these days.

CK: That brings up an interesting topic. Toys. Why use them in your criminal campaign?

WS: Campaign? I'd hardly call it that. Toys are wonderful, don't you agree, Mr. Kent? They're little tiny windows into our youth. They evoke certain . . . memories.

CK: Well, sure. Everyone has a favorite childhood toy they look back on fondly.

WS: Precisely. Pick up an old remote-controlled car or your favorite baby doll that really drinks and wets. You're transported to an innocent time from your past.

CK: You still haven't answered my question, Mr. Schott.

WS: Toyman.

CK: You still haven't answered my question, Toyman.

WS: No, you're just not listening, Mr. Kent. When you hold an old toy in your hands, you're a kid again, for all intents and purposes.

CK: Yes.

WS: And who among us is more vulnerable than a child? What better way to strike, to enact personal revenge, than with an item that renders its target helpless, if only for a moment.

At that point, Schott began to laugh almost uncontrollably. And he kept laughing after I excused myself, after I left his cell, and after I walked down the hallway back to the exit.

This was all a game to him, and I'd become a player, whether I wanted to be or not.

Toyman wanted to enlist Winn in his crazy revenge schemes. It was like he wanted to corrupt Winn to justify his own twisted crimes.

FBI Agent Cameron Chase. Not big on social graces, but you'd be hard-pressed to find someone more determined to get the job done.

Toyman recently died while in prison. His death brought Winn and Winn's mom together for the first time in twenty years. So in that way, Toyman finally did some good in the world.

ALIAS
See individual Martian files

POWERS/ABILITIES
Telepathy; shape-shifting; super-strength; enhanced durability, endurance, and agility; invisibility; intangibility; flight; knowledge of alien cultures; often highly trained soldiers with expert hand-to-hand combat techniques, including Martian fighting styles

HOMEWORLD
Mars

WEAKNESSES
Fire

WHITE MARTIANS

White Martians all but exterminated life on Mars for Green Martians like J'onn J'onzz. So the Martian Manhunter couldn't help but take this attack personally.

Miranda Crane campaigned on hate, proposing a dome around the country to secure it from aliens. When a White Martian attacked her campaign, it only added fuel to her fire.

The White Martian attempted to infiltrate the DEO by using its shapeshifting powers to pose as Miranda Crane. Fortunately, we discovered her ruse, and I was able to team with J'onn to take her down.

MEDICAL REPORT

Report prepared for: Project Supergirl
Name: REDACTED

Condition Update:

It seems our subject has been exposed to the alien element known as kryptonite during her latest skirmish with Supergirl. As a result, her skin has changed its very chemical composition. It has cracked and hardened, becoming a chalky texture prone to flaking.

Meanwhile, her mental state remains more or less a constant. She continues to answer the prompts as coached. Without pause, she declares Supergirl her enemy. Yet I fear with every battle, she is losing conviction.

Blood tests show no apparent sign of future mutation. The kryptonite is still not affecting her. At this point in time, we have no reason to believe that her physical form will be altered further, nor do we suspect that she will be weakened by any further contact with kryptonite. The material simply does not react with her cells the way it does with a true Kryptonian's.

As always, more opportunities to study Supergirl's own physiology would be welcome, if not altogether necessary. We'll await more instructions.

Dr. Beverly Santos

Our girl lacks motivation at the moment. We need to play on her emotions. Use the fact that she looks like a monster now. Twist that hate and point it right back at Supergirl.

ALIAS
No known alias

POWERS/ABILITIES
Mimics Supergirl's power set closely; superstrength, endurance, speed, agility, and durability; freeze, microscopic, x-ray, and telescopic vision; fire breath; flight

HOMEWORLD
Earth

WEAKNESSES
Blue kryptonite

BIZARRO

Maxwell Lord took an innocent girl and turned her into some dark reflection of me. Using a synthesized blue kryptonite bullet, Alex and I were able to take her down, but we couldn't undo what Lord had done. The damage was just too severe.

The Black
Mercy,
courtesy
of Non.

It was everything I ever wanted. But it was all wrong.

Every detail was there. The statue I made for my father. My mother's blue dress. Even the crack on the table where I fell when I was chasing after Aunt Astra. It wasn't just as I remembered it—it was better. A perfect re-creation. Every part of my brain was telling me that I wasn't experiencing some hallucination or a dream. I was actually back on Krypton. And the longer I stayed there, the harder it was to remember my real life. My life on Earth.

I'd find out later that everything I experienced was the result of the Black Mercy plant. The plant was feeding off me, and in exchange, it was making me think I was living out my happiest fantasy. It gave me a world where my mother and father were still alive. Where I could play with little Kal-El, and visit with Aunt Astra like I used to before she was sentenced to the Phantom Zone.

I have no doubt that if it weren't for Alex—if she hadn't used J'onn's mental powers to visit me inside my own mind—I would have died inside my paradise. The Black Mercy would have fed on me until there was nothing left.

But Alex saved me. Because apparently in the Danvers family, that's what sisters do.

To: karadanvers@deomail.com

Cc:

Subject:

Dear Kara,

I know I'm taking the coward's way out by sending you an email rather than saying this to your face, but I need you to hear what I have to say, and I'm not sure I can look you in the eyes and say it. You've lost so much in your life. More than me. Yes, we both lost my—our—dad, but you've also lost your entire planet. Your world. And on top of that, now you've lost your aunt, one of your few living links to Krypton.

It wasn't J'onn that killed Astra. It was me. While you were fighting Non—while you were so angry with him for trapping you inside the world that the Black Mercy plant created—Astra was about to kill J'onn. I couldn't let that happen. So I did what I had to do and stabbed her with a kryptonite sword.

I don't regret it, Kara. I'd do it again in a second to save J'onn, or to save you, or to save anyone I love. But J'onn didn't want something so large to come between us, so he took the blame. And I let him. Because, as I said, I'm a coward.

I hope you can find it in your heart to forgive me. And I hope I can find it in mine to send this message.

I love you,

Alex

Send   ▼   🗑

Alex never sent that email. She didn't have to. She finally broke down and told me everything herself. Just by seeing the regret on her face, I was able to forgive her.

Astra was the family I was born with, but Alex is the family I've chosen.

ALIAS
Carl Draper

POWERS/ABILITIES
Heavily armored alien suit; large arsenal of alien weaponry made with black star alloy; expert hand-to-hand combatant; former Fort Rozz prison guard with extensive training; in-depth knowledge of various alien races and their weaknesses

HOMEWORLD
Trombus

WEAKNESSES
Skewed sense of justice can be manipulated; virtually powerless without his armor

MASTER JAILER

OKAY, SO THIS GUY IS AWESOME. YEAH, SUPER EVIL, AND I'M GLAD SUPERGIRL STOPPED HIM FROM KILLING ALL THE FORMER FORT ROZZ PRISONERS, BUT HE'S ALSO TOTALLY AND COMPLETELY AWESOME. I MEAN, JUST LOOK AT HIS SPACE ARSENAL. BEFORE YOU SAY ANYTHING, SPACE ARSENAL IS COPYRIGHT WINN SCHOTT JR., AND YES, IT WILL BE THE NAME OF MY FUTURE BAND.

ITEM

JAILER'S GUILLOTINE & SUIT

THIS THING IS VICIOUS! A GUILLOTINE STRAIGHT OUT OF THE FRENCH REVOLUTION, IF THE FRENCH REVOLUTION HAD NEAR-INDESTRUCTIBLE ALLOYS AND BLADES SO SHARP YOU COULD USE THEM TO LITERALLY SPLIT HAIRS.

AND HIS SUIT! BLACK STAR ALLOY, ALL THE WAY. MAN, IF I EVER DESIGN ANOTHER COSTUME, I'M TOTALLY GOING TO RIP OFF THE MASTER JAILER'S LOOK. (AT LEAST HIS MASK/ HELMET THINGY.)

THE GUY'S EVEN GOT CHAINS THAT ELONGATE AND SHOOT FROM HIS GAUNTLETS. WHO DOESN'T WANT CHAIN ARMS? TRICK QUESTION. <u>EVERYONE</u> WANTS CHAIN ARMS.

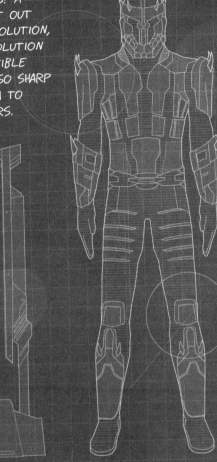

CHAIN ARMS!

Indigo was the one responsible for dislodging my rocket ship and Fort Rozz from the Phantom Zone all those years ago. Imprisoned in Fort Rozz for trying to shut down Krypton's defense system, she used her powers to hack into my ship.

As the most dangerous Fort Rozz inmate, she intended to destroy all of Krypton single-handedly. So when she came to Earth, she brought her genocidal plans with her. She broke into a military base and launched a nuclear strike on National City. I stopped the missile by shutting down its onboard flight computer, while Winn used a computer virus to take down Indigo.

Or at least that's what we thought.

ALIAS
Braniac 8

POWERS/ABILITIES
Able to hack into any electronic systems, including computers and traffic grids; genius-level intellect; can reduce body to nanites and re-form; super-strength, durability, endurance, speed, and agility; able to weaponize her body via claws and elongated appendages

HOMEWORLD
Colu

WEAKNESSES
Her system can be hacked, given the proper resources; susceptible to advanced computer viruses

INDIGO

ALIAS
No known alias

POWERS/ABILITIES
Incredibly intelligent, wealthy, and well-connected in the political, military, and professional worlds; access to powerful Lex Corp technology and Project Cadmus weaponry and employees; possesses armored Lex Corp warsuit

HOMEWORLD
Earth

WEAKNESSES
Human susceptible to conventional attacks

LILLIAN LUTHOR

Luthors seemed destined to clash with members of the House of El. Superman's greatest enemy was arguably Lex Luthor, so it only seems fitting that Lex's mother, Lillian, would become one of my greatest foes as the head of the corrupt clandestin organization known as Project Cadmus.

ALIAS
Hank Henshaw

POWERS/ABILITIES
Cyborg form allows for enhanced strength, endurance, agility, and durability; artificial eye fires blue laser beams; highly connected in the criminal underworld; able to interface with a variety of technology

HOMEWORLD
Earth

WEAKNESSES
Can be overpowered by super-human means

CYBORG SUPERMAN

The original Hank Henshaw was rebuilt by Project Cadmus into something horrific. Already corrupt with a strong anti-alien bias, when Henshaw was granted artificial abilities, he became more dangerous than ever before.

ALIAS
No known alias

POWERS/ABILITIES
Highly trained soldier with advanced weapons and hand-to-hand combat skills; highly connected in the military world

HOMEWORLD
Earth

WEAKNESSES
Human susceptible to conventional attacks

COLONEL JAMES HARPER

I got the distinct feeling that unlike other members of Project Cadmus, Colonel Harper was just doing what he thought was right for his country. Even if he was severely misguided and misinformed.

THE NATIONAL
WHISPER

NEWS   VIDEOS   PHOTOS   SUBSCRIBE

GOT A TIP?

THE NATION'S #1 ALTERNATIVE NEWS SOURCE

WHAT IS PROJECT CADMUS?

By Sergius Hannigan

Have you ever wondered why Superman has never formally aligned himself with the United States government? One would think joining forces with the most powerful country in the world would be beneficial to Superman's goal of keeping the planet safe.

Well, that's exactly what we here at the National Whisper began to ponder, and our subsequent investigation unearthed much more than we bargained for. In fact, we believe we have uncovered the greatest government conspiracy since the faked moon landing or the JFK assassination cover-up. The name of that conspiracy is Project Cadmus.

Believed to be housed in one of the many dummy corporations established as cover for the government's more nefarious goals, Project Cadmus is the flipside of the coin to the Department of Extranormal Operations, a government wing we've reported on in many past articles. Unlike the DEO, which has mainly captured and caged alien threats away from public scrutiny, Project Cadmus goes much further. Their labs are something akin to those of a mad scientist. They study aliens, both violent and peaceful, by any means available to them.

To put it plainly, they cut open aliens to see what makes them tick.
STORY CONTINUED ON FOLLOWING PAGE.

There have been days while working for Cat Grant that I thought the office couldn't be any less hospitable. Between buying multiple lattes for Ms. Grant throughout the course of an afternoon (whenever one reaches anything but its ideal temperature), scheduling appointments and then rescheduling them when Ms. Grant realizes she hasn't told me about a conflicting meeting I was supposed to somehow psychically detect, and arranging for weekly tickets to off-Broadway productions for a mother Ms. Grant can barely tolerate, some days it's hard to imagine things any worse or more hectic.

Then Ms. Grant goes and hires another personal assistant in some bizarre ploy to get us to compete for her affections. Cat Grant is like an honest-to-god supervillain, I kid you not.

Anyway, the name of my friendly competition is Siobhan Smythe, an impossible-to-say Irish name that somehow Ms. Grant pronounced correctly on her first try. Meanwhile, I've been "Kira" for the better part of my employment.

It's not just the fact that Ms. Grant is slowly replacing me right in front of my own face, but there's something . . . off about Siobhan that I just can't put my finger on. She's like nails on a chalkboard. Something about her makes the hairs on my arms stand up.

Okay, enough ranting for one day. After all, I'm sure Ms. Grant's coffee is getting colder as I write this . . .

ALIAS
Siobhan Smythe

POWERS/ABILITIES
Possesses ancient curse of the banshee that grants her a sonic scream capable of concussive sound waves able to shatter solid objects or of propelling her through the air

HOMEWORLD
Earth

WEAKNESSES
Powers can be kept at bay with the use of sound-dampening technology

SILVER BANSHEE

You know, when I think about it, maybe I have some sort of superintuition in addition to my other powers. Because as it turns out, Siobhan is heir to some sort of ancient curse of the banshee. When Cat fired her, she not only became unhinged, but she developed a sonic scream that she tried to use to take revenge against Ms. Grant with the help of Livewire.

I was only able to stop them with a little help from a new friend. A friend not from this planet. Not even from this dimension, in fact.

THE FLASH

ALIAS

Bartholomew Henry "Barry" Allen, the Streak (unofficial)

POWERS/ABILITIES

Can move at superhuman speeds; superfast healing; able to create tornados or other cyclones by moving his limbs at superspeed; can vibrate through solid objects; able to increase the speed in others; able to run so fast he can go back in time; genius-level intellect; highly trained police forensic scientist; access to the geniuses at STAR Labs as well as that institution's vast array of scientific equipment and weaponry

HOMEWORLD

Earth-1

WEAKNESSES

Standard human strength and durability makes him susceptible to a wide variety of attacks; will do almost anything to save his friends and family

When the Flash accidentally jumped from Earth-1 to my Earth, Earth-38, we ended up getting the chance for an old-fashioned superhero team-up (before he zoomed back to his own reality). Not only is Barry a great guy, but we have a lot in common, especially when it comes to being faster than a speeding bullet.

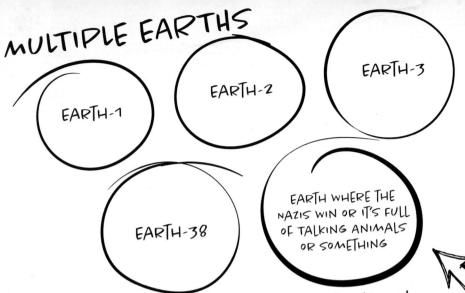

MULTIPLE EARTHS

EARTH-1

EARTH-2

EARTH-3

EARTH-38

EARTH WHERE THE NAZIS WIN OR IT'S FULL OF TALKING ANIMALS OR SOMETHING

Apparently, there are at least 52 worlds all vibrating at different frequencies yet occupying the same space. Barry got into the science behind it a little bit, but I have to admit I was more hung up on the fact that we live on Earth-38.

I mean, seriously, why 38? Why does his Earth get to be number one? Next time I see him, I'm going to demand a recount.

NATIONAL CITY'S WINNING "STREAK"

By Cat Grant

Call him the Red Streak, call him the Blur, or if you must, call him the Flash. But whatever the name of this crimson-clad hero, he's certainly proven himself an ally to National City's resident protector, Supergirl.

I first came in contact with this scarlet speedster when my assistant was knocked from the high-rise offices of CatCo Worldwide Media, plummeting to the ground below and what seemed to be certain death. A red streak like lightning shot through the streets, snatching my assistant in its wake and disappearing as quickly as it had arrived. This was fortunate indeed, as in no time at all, my assistant was back in the offices without a scratch on her, bearing my much-needed afternoon latte. CONTINUED ON PAGE 7B.

The big race. I'm not going to tell you who won. But let's just say this . . . it was close.

Enough time had passed since Astra's death. Non's mourning was over, and he was finally ready to reveal his master plan. I knew something was coming, but I wasn't prepared for Myriad in the least.

Myriad was technology created on Krypton by Aunt Astra. It was designed to force everyone to her way of thinking. It was her misguided attempt to save a dying planet, and the reason my mother banished her to the Phantom Zone in the first place. Simply put, Myriad was a mind-control program.

I found out that Non had activated Myriad in the most awkward way possible, when James and I shared our first kiss. When he didn't react—like at all—I knew something was off. Luckily it wasn't because I'm the galaxy's worst kisser. It was because he, like nearly everyone else in National City, had fallen under Non's mind control.

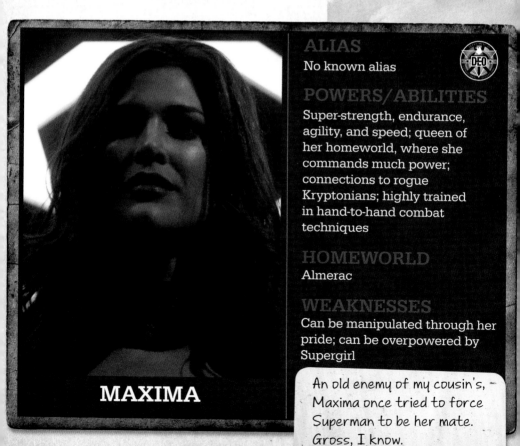

ALIAS
No known alias

POWERS/ABILITIES
Super-strength, endurance, agility, and speed; queen of her homeworld, where she commands much power; connections to rogue Kryptonians; highly trained in hand-to-hand combat techniques

HOMEWORLD
Almerac

WEAKNESSES
Can be manipulated through her pride; can be overpowered by Supergirl

MAXIMA

An old enemy of my cousin's, Maxima once tried to force Superman to be her mate. Gross, I know.

Matters were made worse when a mind-controlled Lucy Lane nearly set all the prisoners at the DEO free. Fortunately, I was able to stop her and incapacitate the freed alien queen, Maxima.

When Indigo captured Alex and defeated J'onn, she and Non forced me to fight my own sister. Armed with the same kryptonite sword that she used to kill Astra, Alex nearly killed me as well. She would have, if not for the last-minute intervention by our mother, Eliza Danvers.

Maxwell Lord and Cat Grant were already equipped with ion blockers to prevent Non's mind control. With their help, I was able to broadcast a message of hope to National City. I'm not sure if it was the S on my uniform, or the words I said, but the people under Myriad's control were able to break free and become themselves again.

But Non and Indigo decided to up Myriad's intensity, broadcasting a steadily increasing frequency that threatened to kill the entire human population on Earth. So J'onn and I took the fight to them at Fort Rozz.

We won, and I flew Fort Rozz into space, finally ending the threat started by my aunt all those years ago.

None of this is how I thought it would go. I mean, have you ever thought about something, anticipated every possibility in your head dozens of times to prepare for every outcome, and then when it happens, it's nothing like you figured it would be?

Well, that in a nutshell is my relationship with one James Olsen.

When I first met James, there was an instant attraction. No heart of steel here. When James was around, my hands would suddenly have no idea where to go, and I'd become this total awkward weirdo who smiled way too much. Like full-on creepy smile.

Even after our first kiss was ruined by mind-controlling aliens—but c'mon, happens to everybody, right?—our first date was like the bad date the heroine goes on at the start of a romantic comedy. You know, the date before she meets the love of her life.

Despite James's original offering of pizza and pot stickers, I was forced to take a rain check when the *Venture* spacecraft launch didn't go quite as planned. When I tried to reschedule with him . . . well, he called my bluff.

Life had been too crazy. Saving the city, fighting criminal alien after criminal alien—when things got quiet, I finally had time to realize that I wasn't the same person I was when James walked into my life. I love him like a friend, but that spark—those weird and awkward feelings—none of it was there anymore.

And maybe it won't ever be there again.

James took this photo of me. I hated the way I looked in it at first, until I realized he was right. This wasn't Kara Danvers, nervous personal assistant. This was _happy_ Kara Danvers, confident and content in the life that she'd made.

D.E.O. NATIONAL CITY HEADQUARTERS

So apparently, the DEO had been holding out on me all this time. While I'd been meeting them at their bunker-like HQ, they had a beautiful building in the heart of the National City that J'onn just didn't feel like telling me about. Now that it's their main operating hub, it'll be quicker for me to get there.

I know, I know. Faster than a speeding bullet and all that. But nobody likes a morning commute.

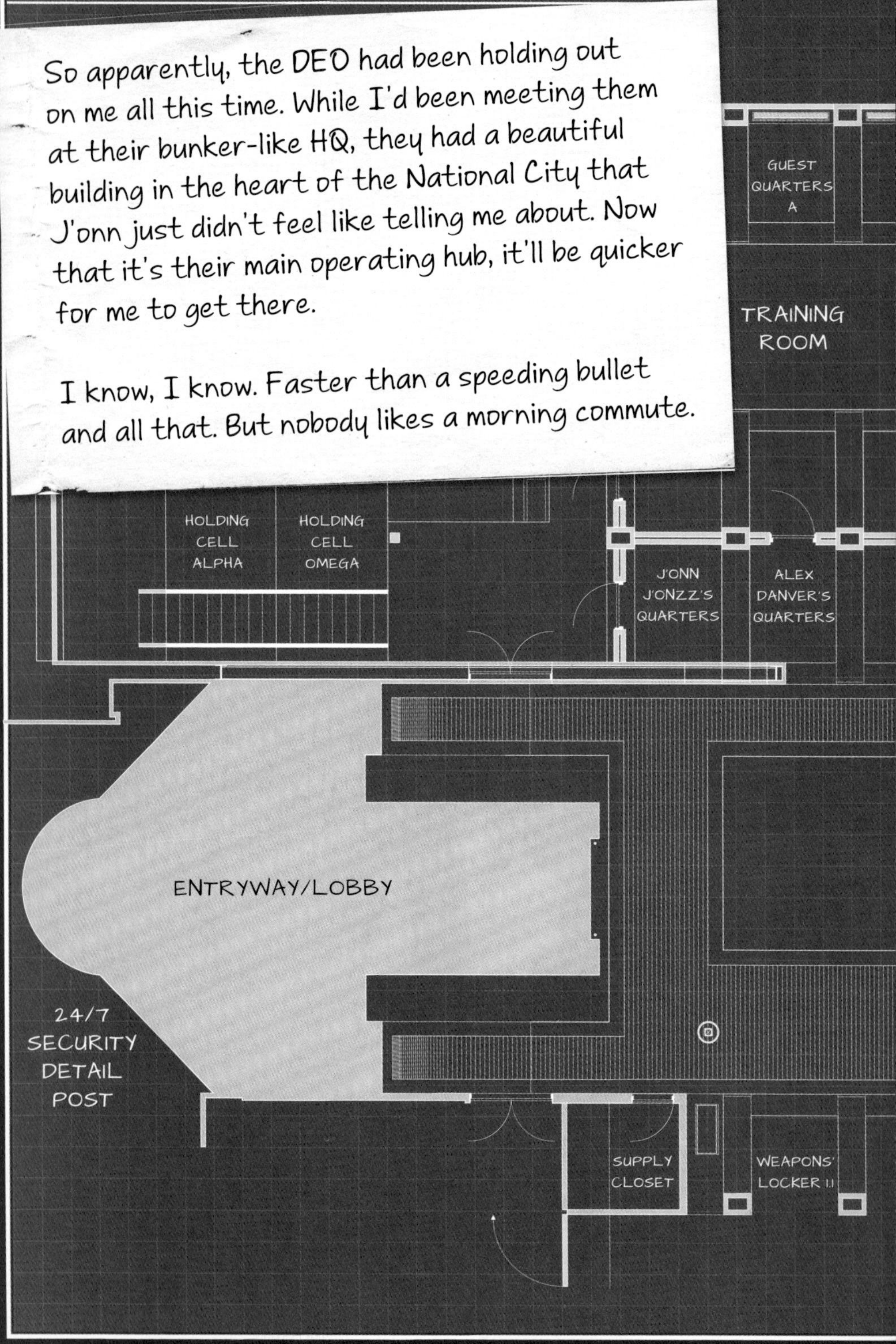

GUEST QUARTERS A

TRAINING ROOM

HOLDING CELL ALPHA

HOLDING CELL OMEGA

J'ONN J'ONZZ'S QUARTERS

ALEX DANVER'S QUARTERS

ENTRYWAY/LOBBY

24/7 SECURITY DETAIL POST

SUPPLY CLOSET

WEAPONS' LOCKER II

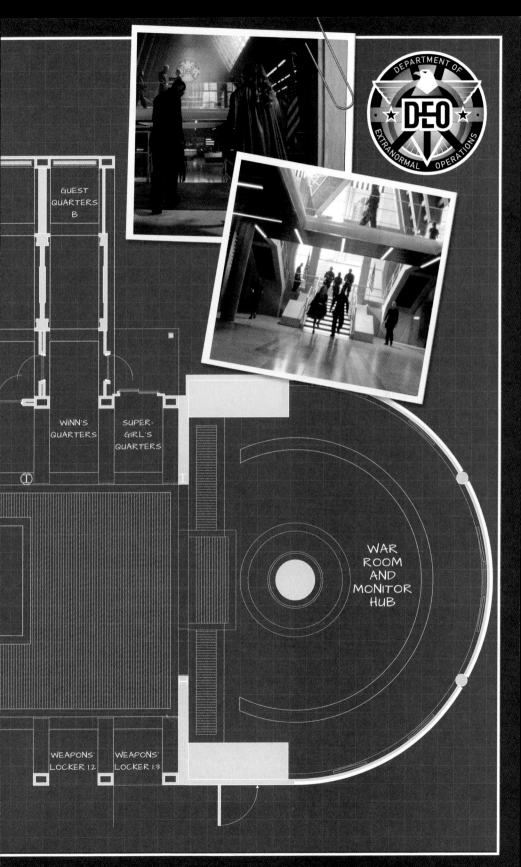

GUEST QUARTERS B

WINN'S QUARTERS

SUPER-GIRL'S QUARTERS

WAR ROOM AND MONITOR HUB

WEAPONS' LOCKER 1.2

WEAPONS' LOCKER 1.3

DEPARTMENT OF EXTRANORMAL OPERATIONS

DEO

ALIAS
Kal-El, Clark Kent

POWERS/ABILITIES
Super-strength, endurance, speed, agility, and durability; heat, microscopic, x-ray, and telepathic vision; accelerated healing; freeze breath; flight

HOMEWORLD
Krypton

WEAKNESSES
Kryptonite, red sun radiation, magic manipulation

SUPERMAN

When I first began my career as Supergirl, Clark noticeably kept his distance. I think my cousin wanted to give me space and not rush in, constantly saving the day as Superman. But after the crisis with Myriad, I guess Clark realized I'd found my voice, so to speak.

When the US spacecraft Venture experienced engine failure and was about to crash back to Earth, Superman and I got the chance for an official team-up. We pooled our strength to save the ship and the passengers onboard.

It was such a fun little family reunion, Clark decided to stick around National City for a while to see what sort of trouble we could get into. And as usual, there was plenty of that to go around.

Kira,

First off, from now on I need to be informed well in advance when Clark Kent is stopping by the office for a visit.

Secondly, all my calls are to be held when Clark is here. No exceptions. I don't care if the rest of the building is on fire or Oprah's walking the halls giving out free hybrids—I don't want to know about it.

Lastly, I know you're not my assistant any longer, but that doesn't help the latte on my desk get any warmer, now does it?

Apparently, Ms. Grant has some sort of long, unrequited crush on my cousin. Something dating back to when the two of them worked together at the *Daily Planet*, I guess. Luckily, with my recent promotion, I could pretty much just ignore this memo – but more on that later!

FORTRESS OF SOLITUDE

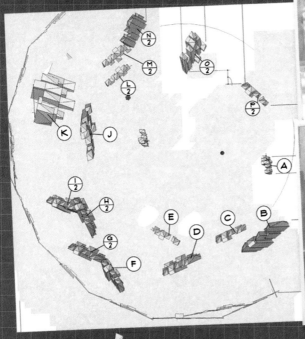

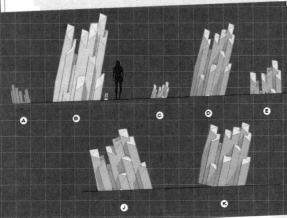

I don't like to be a complainer, and the DEO is nice and all, but man, Clark sure made out like a bandit when it comes to hideouts. The Fortress of Solitude is the perfect Kryptonian getaway for the man who has everything.

Maybe if I bribe Winn with a box of limited-edition action figures or something, he'll build me one . . .

Kelex. A personal service droid prominent on Krypton.

Every clubhouse needs a secret key, and the Fortress of Solitude is no exception. Although this one might look a little conspicuous on Kara Danvers's key chain . . .

The Phantom Zone Projector. On occasion, Kal-El has been forced to go the same route as my mother, using the Phantom Zone to house the ultra-dangerous when no Earthly prison will hold them.

Kryptonite is no fun, but that goes without saying. How so much irradiated rock from Krypton's core landed on Earth in those twenty-four years I was trapped in the Phantom Zone, I'll never know.

The DEO used to stockpile the stuff, but in a gesture of goodwill toward Superman, J'onn finally handed it all over to Clark. It was the right move, even if I can understand how the government would want a fail-safe against rogue Kryptonians.

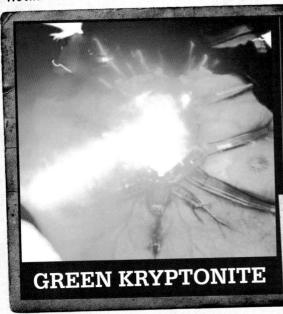

GREEN KRYPTONITE

NOTES
Radioactive material from Krypton's core. Most common variation.

EFFECT ON KRYPTONIANS
Causes weakness, pain, momentary paralysis, and eventual death.

This is the most common type of kryptonite, so of course it's the kind that hurts me the most. Wouldn't want life on Earth to get too easy for its resident superheroes, now would we?

BLUE KRYPTONITE

NOTES
Synthesized by the DEO to specifically target Bizarro clones. (SEE: Bizarro.)

EFFECT ON KRYPTONIANS
Harmless to natural Kryptonians. Causes weakness, pain, momentary paralysis, and eventual death in Bizarro clones.

I hated that blue kryptonite was used on Bizarro, but there was no other choice. I only hope that we can give her a normal life someday

NOTES

Created by Maxwell Lord in an attempt to stop invading Kryptonians. (SEE: Maxwell Lord.)

EFFECT ON KRYPTONIANS

Causes drastic personality changes, making subject more hostile; unleashes inner rage involuntarily.

RED KRYPTONITE

I'd rather not relive this one, if that's okay with you. I'm not crazy about being reminded that red kryptonite messed with my mind so much that I dropped Cat Grant off a building and nearly killed her.

NOTES

Unleashed by Rhea, the Daxamite queen. (SEE: Rhea.)

EFFECT ON KRYPTONIANS

Causes fear-based hallucinations, forcing the subject to see his or her worst nightmare and lash out at the fictional target.

SILVER KRYPTONITE

When exposed to silver kryptonite, Superman believed I was Zod, arguably his deadliest enemy. Let's just say I was lucky to walk away from that fight. (As was Clark.)

It may be altogether possible that I have too many options on my plate. Let me explain.

Recently, Ms. Grant decided I had graduated past the role of her personal assistant. Not only was I not fired, as—let's be honest—I figured was a given since day one, but I was given the proverbial golden ticket. Cat said I could have any job I wanted. That sort of thing just doesn't happen to people.

So for the last few days, I've been making lists and throwing away those lists and then making more lists, trying to judge my own strengths and weaknesses. Through all of it, one thing keeps coming back to me: reporter.

I know, I know! It sounds like I'm just copying Clark. I've told myself that a thousand times. But that doesn't make the idea fade away. Clark and I have a lot in common, and exposing the truth and striving for justice in the world are two of the big ones. Maybe it's in House of El blood. Maybe it's another side effect of yellow sun radiation.

Either way, I think I've made my choice.

Kara Danvers, news reporter for CatCo Worldwide Media.

Can't wait to see that on a business card.

Oh gosh! I need to get business cards!

Eve Teschmacher, or as everyone at CatCo knows her, "MISS TESCHMACHER!" Ms. Grant really has some pipes on her when she's annoyed at her assistants. Now imagine that with superhearing. Yeah, not ideal.

My new boss at CatCo magazine, Snapper Carr. Originally, he didn't want an amateur like me around, and treated me like dirt. Later, things got better between us. I mean, yeah, he still treated me terribly and didn't want me around, but at least he published my articles. So, win?

LENA LUTHOR

ALIAS
No known alias

POWERS/ABILITIES
Owner of L-Corp, with access
to its technological innovations
and often-brilliant staff; owner
of CatCo Worldwide Media;
well-connected in politics and
business; close personal friend
of Supergirl

HOMEWORLD
Earth

WEAKNESSES
Human susceptible to conventional attacks

The Luthor name certainly
carries some weight with it.
They're one of the wealthiest
families on the planet, but the
Luthors are also known to
be some of the most corrupt.
You'd be hard-pressed to find
someone who doesn't know the
legacy of the nefarious Lex
Luthor.

This is the burden that Lena Luthor is forced to bear every
single day of her life. I'll admit that when I first met her, I
wasn't sure what to think, either. But now she's become one
of my best friends. Lucky for me, she's as fiercely loyal to her
friends as she is to her many businesses.

L

CORP

Press Release

Luthor Corp is now L-Corp! The changing face of the future of National City.

NATIONAL CITY – One of the world's most important corporations and largest employers is evolving with the times. While the Luthor Corp name has come to mean so much to so many people—as a source of employment, a trusted manufacturer, and a strategic partner—the company has been tarnished in recent years by the actions of former CEO Lex Luthor. In an effort to reestablish itself as a positive force in the world, a global juggernaut as charitable as it is profitable, Luthor Corp has become L-Corp, leading American business into a new future.

CEO Lena Luthor had this to say about the momentous news:

"My brother hurt a lot of good, innocent people. My family owes a debt. Not just to Metropolis, but to everyone. And I intend to pay that. By renaming my company L-Corp, we will usher in a new age of cooperation and community. Together we will chart a brighter future."

L-Corp. Same global leader. New global vision.

From day one, Lena Luthor was the black sheep of the Luthor family. An illegitimate child of her father, Lionel Luthor, she was shunned fairly early on by her new mother, Lillian. Nevertheless, Lena found a friend in her new brother, Lex, but she couldn't have predicted the monster he'd grow up to become.

Lena was nothing like the woman who raised her. Lillian kept Lena at arm's length, always letting her know in subtle ways that she did not truly belong.

THE NATION'S #1 ALTERNATIVE NEWS SOURCE

LIONEL LUTHOR'S ILLEGITIMATE LOVE CHILD?

By Regal Simonson

Influential billionaire and known socialite Lionel Luthor has always had his share of secrets. However, none may be bigger than the reported bombshell he dropped on his wife Lillian this week, when he introduced their new daughter to the world. While the official word is that four-year-old Lena Luthor was adopted in an effort to give back to the community, sources close to the Luthor family say that Lena is actually Lionel Luthor's secret love child, born out of wedlock. Those same sources claim that Lillian is taking the news rather well, considering the circumstances.

Is there more trouble in the Luthor household than previously reported? For now, we can only sit back and wait for the other $2,000 shoe to drop.

ALIAS
John Corben

POWERS/ABILITIES
Superhuman strength, endurance, agility, and durability; kryptonite heart capable of firing blasts of kryptonite radiation

HOMEWORLD
Earth

WEAKNESSES
Cannot function without his artificial heart

METALLO

John Corben didn't just hate L-Corp; he also had a severe mad-on for all things Kryptonian. He became the perfect subject for Project Cadmus, and they revamped the hitman into Metallo, a powerful killer with a Kryptonian heart.

Hired by Lex Luthor to murder his sister, Lena, hitman John Corben first attempted to crash the *Venture* spacecraft, which was supposed to be carrying Lena as a passenger. Next, he used drones in an attempt to shoot down her helicopter. Clark and I were on hand for that one, too, and made sure Lena was safe.

Corben is a professional, though, so he tried one last time at L-Corp's renaming ceremony. There, Lena shot him, proving herself just as capable as her brother.

ALIAS
No known alias

POWERS/ABILITIES
Genius-level intellect; expert computer hacker and engineer; innovative inventor raised by the notorious Winslow Schott Sr. (SEE: Toyman.)

HOMEWORLD
Earth

WEAKNESSES
Human susceptible to conventional attacks

WINN SCHOTT JR.

Realizing he was wasting his potential as the IT guy for CatCo, Winn followed his admittedly boyish sense of adventure and got a job working for the DEO. It wasn't hard to convince J'onn that Winn could be an asset to the team.

Winn's design for anti-kryptonite armor. Pretty easily destroyed by the Metallos, but the armor bought us enough extra time for Alex and J'onn to join the fight.

Cadmus had fired the first shot. Even though we stopped the Metallos, something more frightening became clear. I was at war, and I didn't even know whom exactly I was fighting.

It's hard not to be intimidated when you walk into Lena Luthor's office. But it's not her high-rise view of West Cordova Street, her stern-faced secretary, or even her expensive taste in office décor that takes one aback. It's her very presence.

Lena Luthor is almost the exact opposite of her infamous brother, Lex. While she commands a room just as naturally, she does so in a welcoming way. Her smile beams with sincerity, her eyes are alight with optimism. If I were a photographer with an eye for capturing the true personality of a person, I would have snapped dozens of shots as soon as Lena brought out her company's new alien detection device. This is who Lena Luthor is. Someone truly excited to share ideas with the world.

Even if those ideas might be controversial.

The alien detector she took out of a nifty locked safe was about the size of a computer mouse. And like a computer, it contains within it the possibility to do great evil in the world, or perhaps great good. Lena certainly views it as the latter.

With a simple touch of a finger, Lena's alien detection device can determine if said finger belongs to a human being or to a visitor from another planet. The marketability for such a device is enormous, and its potential uses range from screening incapacitated patients at hospitals to allowing potential employers to know exactly what kind of being they're hiring. The morality of the device is a different thing altogether, and a concept Lena has obviously thought much about.

"Aliens want to be citizens; that's now their right," says Ms. Luthor. "But if humans want to know which of their fellow citizens aren't actually one of them, then that's their right, too."

CONTINUED ON PAGE 33.

ALIAS
No known alias

POWERS/ABILITIES
Enhanced strength and durability; able to shapeshift into almost anything; highly connected in politics and the metahuman worlds; natural leader

HOMEWORLD
Durla

WEAKNESSES
Susceptible to conventional attacks

PRESIDENT OLIVIA MARSDIN

It's not every day that you get to meet the president of the United States of America. I'd guess saving her from an onslaught of fireballs probably happens even less often.

But either way, I got to meet the president. And she didn't die or anything!

Go, Supergirl!

CATCO

MAGAZINE

GIVE ME
YOUR TIRED,
YOUR POOR,
YOUR HUDDLED
MASSES.
YOUR ALIENS.

NSIDE:

THE PRESIDENT
DRAWS AN
INTERGALACTIC
LINE IN THE SAND

4509 00500 2

We later discovered that
the president was an alien, a
shapeshifter from the planet
Durla. Kind of explains why
she was so invested in people
like me.

Scorcher first attacked when President Marsdin arrived in National City. While I wasn't able to apprehend her then, I did catch up to her when she struck again as the president signed the Alien Amnesty Act, a document that would grant rights to those from other worlds.

Scorcher believed the act was just a way to register aliens so that they could be targeted. She clung to that cynical worldview even after we took her into custody.

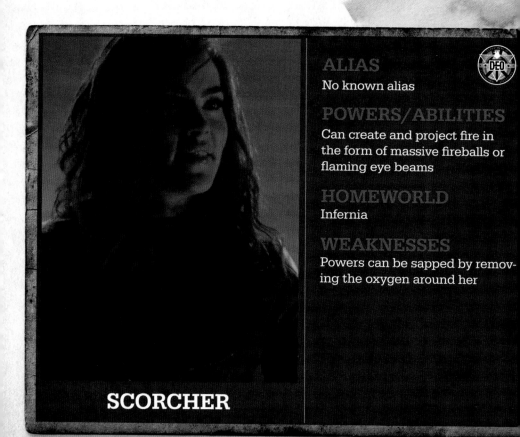

ALIAS
No known alias

POWERS/ABILITIES
Can create and project fire in the form of massive fireballs or flaming eye beams

HOMEWORLD
Infernia

WEAKNESSES
Powers can be sapped by removing the oxygen around her

SCORCHER

ALIAS
No known alias

POWERS/ABILITIES
Works for the National City Police Department's Science Division, with access to files on alien life forms and other weird phenomena; highly trained hand-to-hand combatant; excellent markswoman

HOMEWORLD
Earth

WEAKNESSES
Human susceptible to conventional attacks

MAGGIE SAWYER

Detective Maggie Sawyer came into my sister's life while President Marsdin was visiting National City. Alex originally lied about what branch of the government she worked for, but the two became good friends anyway—and they constantly ran into each other on some of our city's weirder cases.

It took some time, but they finally began to date. Their relationship easily became the most serious of my sister's life.

Hey Mags

What do you want?

What makes you think I want anything? Can't I just text my girlfriend when I'm feeling lonely?

No. You definitely want something.

You only call me Mags when you're asking for a favor.

I really don't appreciate the tone.

There's no tone. This is a text. You can't hear my tone.

A tone is a tone.

Okay, fine. What's up?

...

Could you pick up a pint of ice cream on your way over?

I KNEW IT!

What?

I knew you wanted something!

So that's a hard no on the ice cream then?

Sigh.

What flavor?

ALIAS
Mike Matthews

POWERS/ABILITIES
Superstrength that allows for leaping long distances; enhanced endurance, speed, agility, and durability; accelerated healing; possesses Legion flight ring that allows for flight; trained in combat techniques by Supergirl; access to 31st-century technology

HOMEWORLD
Daxam

WEAKNESSES
Lead (formerly)

MON-EL

Kryptonians and the alien race Daxamites have a long history. None of it is good. I have to admit I had a slight, teeny tiny, minuscule prejudice against Mon-El when he first learned he was a Daxamite.

Okay, so I may have punched him a few times.

But getting past those stereotypes and really getting to know Mon-El was one of the best things I've ever done.

Daxam was destroyed by debris from Krypton's own destruction. What I didn't know at the time was that Mon-El was a prince from his homeworld, sent to Earth thanks to a faithful friend.

When Mon-El originally crash-landed here in a Kryptonian pod, we understandably mistook him for one of my people. Daxamites have similar powers as Kryptonians here on Earth, but are immune to kryptonite. So he had that going for him.

APPLICATION FOR EMPLOYMENT

APPLICANT INFORMATION

LAST NAME: MATTHEWS **FIRST NAME:** MIKE **M.I.:** K.E.

DATE: SURE, WHY NOT?

STREET ADDRESS: I'M VERY INTERESTED IN GETTING ONE OF THESE.

CITY: NATIONAL CITY **STATE:** EARTH. EARTH IS A STATE, RIGHT?

ZIP: IS THIS A PERSONAL QUESTION? IT FEELS LIKE IT'S A PERSONAL QUESTION.

PHONE: I TRIED, BUT DAXAM IS LIKE SUPER FAR AWAY.

EMAIL: MALE. DEFINITELY MALE. **DATE AVAILABLE:** IMMEDIATELY. AS I WRITE THIS EVEN.

SOCIAL SECURITY NO: SOCIAL SECURITY YES!

DESIRED SALARY: I DON'T KNOW. IS A MILLION EARTH DOLLARS A FAIR AMOUNT?

POSITION APPLIED FOR: THE PRESTIGIOUS ROLE OF INTERN TO ALL OF CATCO WORLDWIDE MEDIA.

ARE YOU LEGALLY ELIGIBLE TO WORK IN THE US? UM . . . LET'S GO WITH YES.

HAVE YOU EVER WORKED FOR THIS COMPANY BEFORE? NOPE.

HAVE YOU EVER BEEN CONVICTED OF A FELONY? NOT ON THIS PLANET, NO.

In an attempt to give Mon-El a normal life here on Earth, I got him a job as an intern at CatCo. Needless to say, I had immediate regrets.

As Supergirl, I had better luck training Mon-El to use his powers. It took a while, but Mon-El finally started to take his responsibilities seriously.

Did I mention it took a while? I feel like I should repeat that for emphasis.

For lack of a better name (because I'm pretty sure it doesn't have a name at all), let's call this glamorous destination the "alien dive bar." Because that's what it is. A place where aliens can find a little slice of home on Earth. Or a little drink from home, at least.

Maggie introduced Alex to this place even before they were dating. It quickly became the DEO's after-work bar of choice.

ALIAS
M'gann M'orzz

POWERS/ABILITIES
Telepathy; shapeshifting; superstrength; enhanced durability, endurance, and agility; invisibility; intangibility; knowledge of alien cultures; adept at hand-to-hand combat; knowledge of Martian fighting techniques

HOMEWORLD
Mars

WEAKNESSES
Fire

MISS MARTIAN

For years, J'onn thought that he was the last Green Martian. Then he met Miss Martian while she was bartending at the alien dive bar. J'onn was later shocked to learn that M'gann was actually a White Martian in disguise, one who had rejected the cruelty of her people for the more benevolent ideals of Green Martian life.

After crashing and burning as an intern at CatCo, Mon-El found bartending more to his speed.

ALIAS
Veronica Sinclair

POWERS/ABILITIES
Extremely well-connected in the criminal, business, and political worlds; natural showman with a flair for the dramatic; access to dozens of alien lackeys

HOMEWORLD
Earth

WEAKNESSES
Human susceptible to conventional attacks

ROULETTE

National City earned its own alien underground fight club when a criminal named Roulette used her connections to pit alien vs. alien for the amusement of the city's scuzziest rich and powerful.

YOU ARE CORDIALLY INVITED TO A

Roulette Arena Event

FRIDAY AT MIDNIGHT
17 JOHNS WAY

FEATURING THE BATTLE OF THE MARTIANS
A DEATH MATCH BETWEEN THE LAST TWO SURVIVING GREEN MARTIANS

DISCRETION IS MANDATORY. VIOLATORS WILL BE DEALT WITH.
SEVERELY.

One of Roulette's toughest champions, Draaga—a fierce alien hell-bent on killing a Kryptonian. Spoiler alert: he didn't.

I later helped shut down Roulette's slavery ring on the planet Maaldoria. It seems this woman isn't happy unless she's doing something disgusting.

ALIAS

James Olsen

POWERS/ABILITIES

Expert hand-to-hand combatant; wears hi-tech armored suit and shield; possesses keen detective skills; highly connected in the metahuman community; partnered with Winn Schott Jr., with access to Schott's technological advancements and communication gear

HOMEWORLD

Earth

WEAKNESSES

Human susceptible to conventional attacks when not prepared

GUARDIAN

You turn a blind eye in your friends' direction for one second, and all of a sudden they become a secret vigilante duo. While James Olsen does make an impressive crime fighter even without powers, and Winn is more than capable of supplying him information in the field, it took some getting used to when I first learned about National City's new "Guardian."

The DEO Speed Wagon. Yes, Winn named it.

GUARDIAN'S SUIT

FIRST, I'M JUST GOING TO SAY THAT NOT TELLING KARA IS A MISTAKE.
SECOND, WE SHOULD TOTALLY TELL KARA.
THIRD, HERE'S MY PRELIMINARY DESIGN FOR THE SUIT.
(DID I MENTION WE SHOULD TELL KARA?)

MASK IS MADE OF LEAD SO SUPERGIRL CAN'T DETECT YOUR SECRET IDENTITY. EVEN THOUGH IT WOULD BE TOTALLY EASIER FOR ME IF YOU JUST TOLD KARA. ALSO, YOU OWE ME. LIKE BIG TIME.

SHIELD IS MADE OF TITANIUM ALLOY. IT'LL STOP MORE THAN A BULLET, I GUARANTEE IT.
PLUS IT FOLDS OUT OF YOUR GAUNTLET. IT'S LIKE COMBAT ORIGAMI. YOU'RE WELCOME.

When the camera James's father gave him was broken due to some thoughtless criminals, James was inspired to take the law into his own hands.

Winn and the Guardian earned a third partner when an alien Winn was dating named Lyra Strayd leant her incredible strength to their team's efforts.

PARASITE

ALIAS
Dr. Rudy Jones

POWERS/ABILITIES
Contaminated with an alien parasite that gave him the ability to feed off the energy of others, weakening his prey while gaining himself sustenance; superhuman strength, endurance, durability, and agility; able to absorb powers from those targets he drains

HOMEWORLD
Earth

WEAKNESSES
System can be overtaxed when forced to absorb powerful radioactive materials like plutonium

After uncovering a perfectly preserved 5,000-year-old wolf, Dr. Rudy Jones was infected with a murderous alien parasite. Alex and J'onn located him and took him back to the DEO.

That's when things went from bad to worse.

Svalbard, Norway. Thorul Arctic Research Station.

8.42 PM
Still not at one hundred percent. I'm so cold, but I shouldn't push myself. That alien . . . parasite . . . if it did infect me, it was less than three hours ago. No way to be sure. Can't remember the incident at all. Why can't I remember?

I should eat something. I'm so hungry. Did I skip dinner? Maybe I could take a break and feed. Will continue these notes when I return.

9:54 PM
I did all this, didn't I? All of them. Dead. The whole station. I'm the only survivor. But I'm so, so hungry. Wait. I'm hearing something. Outside. An aircraft. Someone is coming. I should warn them, but . . . I should feed first.

So cold. So hungry. I should feed.

Jones mutated when J'onn and I confronted him. He absorbed both our energies at the same time, truly becoming a Parasite. Fortunately for me, the sun healed my wounds. J'onn wasn't so lucky. He needed a blood transfusion to recover.

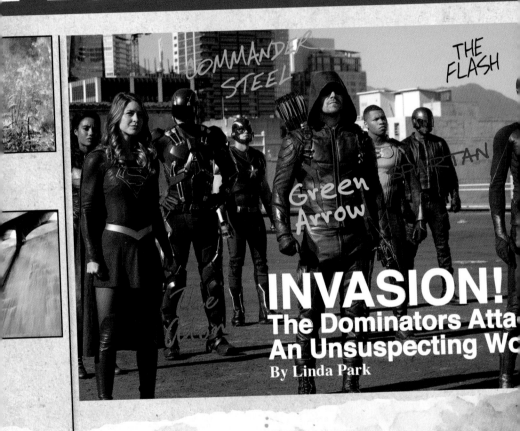

Central City
Picture News

COMMANDER STEEL

THE FLASH

Green Arrow

SPARTAN

The Atom

INVASION!
The Dominators Atta
An Unsuspecting Wo

By Linda Park

I went to Earth-1 and all I got was this lousy newspaper.

(And, like, the best team-up adventure of all time!)

The hostile aliens called the Dominators had first been spotted on Earth-1 in the 1950s, but when they reared their toothy heads again, the Flash zapped to my Earth with his teammate, Cisco Ramon, and recruited me to defend their planet.

Apparently, Cisco is sort of like Barry Allen's own personal Winn, except he can interface with other dimensions as the hero Vibe. (Winn would be sooooo jealous.)

This stick-in-the-mud is called Green Arrow. It took a while for Star City's famous archer to warm up to me, but he did. I have that effect on people. It's a talent, really.

The White Canary. The leader of a team called the Legends. They fight crime by traveling through time. Seriously!

Felicity Smoak. Team Arrow's resident computer expert and total sweetheart. We barely got to talk, but I have a feeling she's my favorite.

Wild Dog. I guess he's just a guy with a gun and a hockey mask? Either way, not pleasant.

Ragman seemed nice and all, and I know Green Arrow trusts him, but he kinda gave me the heebie-jeebies. I know, I need to be better as a person. But you didn't hear him talk . . .

We barely met, but Mr. Terrific seemed super smart and funny. Team Arrow certainly isn't worse off having a member who's actually friendly.

For a world that doesn't have its own Superman, Commander Steel is doing his best to fill that void. He can turn to metal, so maybe he's taking the whole Man of Steel thing too literally?

John Diggle aka Spartan. Green Arrow's right-hand man, and totally involved in a Team Arrow Bromance I'd rather not get into.

Vixen can summon animal powers whenever she wants, and there is no part of that that isn't awesome.

The Atom. Ray Palmer. He can shrink! Like, for real. Sort of reminds me of Clark in a way I can't really explain.

Firestorm is actually two people: Professor Martin Stein and Jefferson Jackson. If you listen closely, you can actually hear him argue with himself. It's really funny in a creepy way.

Green Arrow's kid sister even got in on the Dominator-fighting action. She calls herself Speedy, and is nearly as good as her brother. Plus, she's way nicer.

Through the use of a pain-inflicting device created by Martin Stein, and tons of metahumans kicking Dominator heinie in unison, we managed to save Earth-1.

And I was totally serious and didn't have a stupid grin on my face the entire time because so many superheroes teaming up isn't the greatest thing on any Earth. (If you've read this book this far, you know that none of that last sentence is true.)

Very few people trust a Luthor. So when Metallo interrupted the trial of Lillian Luthor, it was pretty easy for Cadmus to frame Lena in the process.

NATIONAL CITY ARREST/DISPOSITION REPORT
National City Police Department

NCIC:NaC209

DEFENDANT IDENTIFICATION

LAST NAME	FIRST NAME		
LUTHOR	LENA		

STREET ADDRESS	CITY	ZIP
1961 SCHAFFENBERGER WAY SUITE 23	NATIONAL CITY	90742

PHONE NUMBER	SOCIAL SECURITY NUMBER
(714) 555-5878	████████████

DRIVERS LICENSE	EMPLOYER/OCCUPATION
███████████	CEO OF L-CORP

SEX	RACE	DATE OF BIRTH	HAIR
F	WHITE	10/24/93	DARK BROWN

EYES	WEIGHT	HEIGHT	PLACE OF ARREST
GREEN	135 LBS.	5' 5½"	L-CORP HEADQUARTERS

ARRESTING OFFICER	DATE OF ARREST	TIME OF ARREST
DETECTIVE MAGGIE SAWYER	2/13	7:18

	CHARGE DESCRIPTION	
1.	AIDING AND ABETTING A FELON	
2.	ACCESSORY AFTER THE FACT	
3.	CONSPIRACY	

RIGHT THUMBPRINT

FACTS OF ARREST

SUSPECT WAS CAUGHT ON A SECURITY TAPE HANDLING KRYPTONITE THAT WAS USED TO POWER PRISONER JOHN CORBEN (METALLO)'S CYBERNETIC BODY, ALLOWING HIM TO ATTACK THE TRIAL OF LILLIAN LUTHOR, LENA'S MOTHER. AS THE ONLY VISITOR TO THE PRISON THE PREVIOUS EVENING, IT IS BELIEVED THAT LENA LUTHOR HANDED THE CONTRABAND KRYPTONITE TO CORBEN AND ENABLED THE SUBSEQUENT ATTACK.

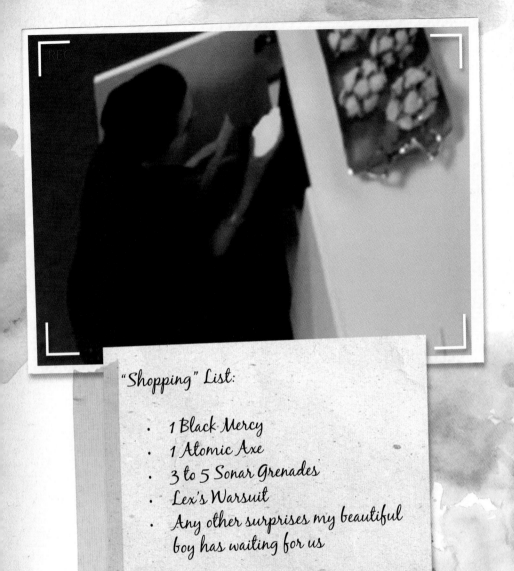

"Shopping" List:

- 1 Black Mercy
- 1 Atomic Axe
- 3 to 5 Sonar Grenades
- Lex's Warsuit
- Any other surprises my beautiful boy has waiting for us

As it turned out, Lillian was once again using her daughter, this time to get into one of Lex Luthor's secure weapon caches. The cache had quite a few things Lillian wanted on her continued mission to rid the world of aliens, and by using Metallo to spring her daughter from prison, she had Lena up against a wall.

In the end, the artificial kryptonite proved unstable, exploding and taking John Corben with it.

ALIAS
No known alias

POWERS/ABILITIES
5th-dimensional imp with near-omnipotent magical powers and near-unlimited knowledge

HOMEWORLD
The 5th Dimension

WEAKNESSES
Must return to his homeworld if he's tricked into spelling or saying his name backward

MXYZPTLK

Dearest Diary,

It is I, the beautiful and divine Supergirl. While it's hard being the only woman on planet Earth worth much of anything, things have been wonderful lately. You see, I've met my future husband, Mr. Mxyzptlk.

I can't say enough good things about him. His omnipotent powers, his charming smile, the way he can force mortals to commit his every minor whim with just a wave of his hand. It's all so dreamy. Much better than that McGurk-El moron with whom I continue to waste my time. Did I mention that Mxy is quite dashing? And smart, too. Why, I doubt I've met a more intelligent—

Oops. Guess this journal entry is going to be cut short. But I'll be sure to write back in a few months with more on how Mr. Mxyzptlk is just simply wonderful.

AHH!

KLTPZYXM!!!!

I came home from work one day to find Mr. Mxyzptlk writing in my journal and wearing one of my bathrobes. Mxyzptlk wrote his own name backward and disappeared back to the 5th dimension before I could let him know exactly what I think about unwanted visitors.

And hey, I don't really sound like this, do I?

Dear Diary,

Mon-El is arrogant, stubborn, unmotivated, and the last person on Earth my parents would want me to be with. And to make matters worse, I think I've fallen in love with him.

He's all of those things I mentioned. That's true. But he's also this genuinely kind, sweet, good person under all the Daxamite bravado and that insultingly perfect smile. He might see himself as the grand conquering hero, but really he's this goofball puppy, one who makes me laugh every single day, whether I'm in the mood to or not.

So we went ahead and decided to try this out. Sure, we've already had our share of near-death experiences and interruptions from arrogant magical beings from advanced dimensions, but it looks like things are finally lining up in our favor.

I'm just really happy. That's all. I'm really, really happy. Now if you'll excuse me, I'm going to go and find everything in my apartment made of wood and knock on it at superspeed.

WELCOME

Kara Danvers's Blog

National News from the National City

*This blog represents the personal thoughts and opinions of reporter Kara Danvers and is in no way affiliated with CatCo Worldwide Media.

Without a witness on record to corroborate my account, Snapper wouldn't publish my warning of Cadmus's all-out war against aliens. So I had to take matters into my own hands and publish it on my blog. In doing so, I violated my noncompete clause with CatCo, and lost the only job I ever really loved.

blog post #064:

URGENT – CADMUS HAS STOLEN THE ALIEN REGISTRY
ALL ALIENS NEED TO PROTECT THEMSELVES

By Kara Danvers

According to an eyewitness report from Supergirl, the clandestine Cadmus agency has stolen an alien registry belonging to the United States government in an attempt to round up aliens living on Earth for nefarious purposes. Dozens of missing persons cases have already been filed across the country. Many of these missing individuals are believed to be in the custody of the Cadmus organization.

The NCPD asks the general public for assistance in locating these missing aliens and to report any information about these kidnappings to their crime tip hotline.

To assist in their investigation, Supergirl and authorities request witnesses please keep their facts in all crime tip accounts clear and concise, including where, when, how, and what. If the information provided is credible to Supergirl's search, tipsters may be eligible for a cash reward. Any information that the public can provide will be greatly appreciated.

"Cadmus's anti-alien immigration and interplanetary xenophobia has fueled paranoia and distrust in our community," Supergirl says. "Their fear-mongering tactics and illegal activity openly defy the basic principles of our American democracy and Constitution and threaten to destroy the very fabric of our society, which not only thrives but flourishes because of its vibrant diversity."

If you have information on any missing persons cases, alien or otherwise, please call the NCPD at (714) 555-NCPD.

ALIAS
No known alias

POWERS/ABILITIES
Supernatural ability to place victims into a shared dream world while simultaneously placing them in comas; controls reality of manufactured dream world; teleportation; able to steal the powers of his victims; seemingly omnipotent knowledge (and perhaps abilities)

HOMEWORLD
Unknown

WEAKNESSES
Unknown

MUSIC MEISTER

I just returned from a weird dream world
Where people sang and danced on a whim.
It was created by a being named the Music Meister,
All for the amusement of him.

It was a strange place that I went to, for sure
While I lay asleep there in bed.
Flash was with me, as were foes,
All singing inside of my head.

We had to come to terms with our loves
And solve the plot of a play
With gangsters and guns and familiar friends
Helping us chart out the way.

In the end, I discovered that I
Was indeed in love with Mon-El.
We woke back on Earth ready to send
The Music Meister right back to . . . where he came from.

There. That's better. Think I got that out of my system.

ALIAS
No known alias

POWERS/ABILITIES
Super-strength that allows for leaping long distances; enhanced endurance, speed, agility, and durability; accelerated healing; highly trained in hand-to-hand combat and Daxam fighting styles; commands entire army of powerful armed Daxamites

HOMEWORLD
Daxam

WEAKNESSES
Lead

QUEEN RHEA

As it turned out, Mon-El wasn't the only person to escape Daxam with his life. His parents, the king and queen of Daxam, had been hunting for him for months, alongside what essentially amounted to an army of Daxamites.

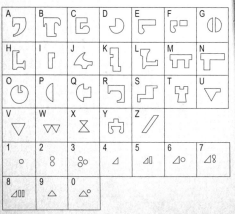

I know it's normal for people not to get along with the parents of their significant other, but I doubt many people have their boyfriend's mom put out an intergalactic bounty on their head.

That's how much Rhea didn't like her son, the prince of Daxam, dating a "filthy" Kryptonian like me. Yeah, that's not offensive.

Mon-El was able to talk some sense into his father, King Lar Gand. But while we didn't know it at the time, Lar was then murdered by Rhea. She believed her husband had committed the ultimate sin. That he had betrayed her.

It was safe to say, things were not looking up.

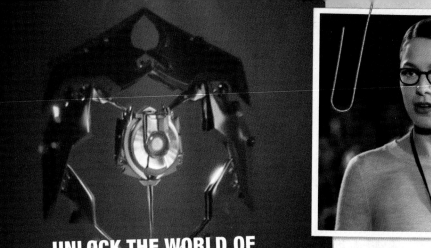

UNLOCK THE WORLD OF
BIOMAX

The Nanobot Medical Miracle

FROM
JACK
SPHEER

SPHEERICAL INDUSTRIES

I had the opportunity to attend a press event for Jack Spheer, the CEO of Spheerical Industries, who just happened to be Lena Luthor's ex-flame. But what started as a puff piece for my blog turned out way bigger than either of us figured.

It turned out that Jack's CFO, Beth Breen, was controlling her boss, using his own nanobot technology against him. Lena was forced to deactivate the bots, essentially killing Jack to save my life.

CATCO
MAGAZINE

SPHEERICAL
STOPS MOVING

By Snapper Carr
and Kara Danvers

Supergirl has made the cover of countless newspapers and magazines, but none of that compares to this, the first Kara Danvers byline, and the very scoop that got me my reporter job back at CatCo.

ALBATROSS BAY PRISON

SECURITY
OBSERVATION

FRONT VIEW

MAIN ENTRANCE AND
GUARD STATION

CELL BLOCK A

CELL BLOCK B

ABOVE VIEW

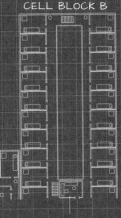

INDIVIDUAL
CONTAINMENT CELLS

SECURITY STATION
AND CHECKPOINT

SECURITY STATION
AND CHECKPOINT

Rick Malverne

An old face from Midvale who had figured out my secret identity. He tried to blackmail me into freeing his father from prison by holding Alex as his own prisoner.

Luckily, Rick's father didn't quite see eye-to-eye with his son. He gave up Alex's location, and I was able to save her at the last second.

TAKING BACK THE NATION

By Cat Grant

I do not like science-fiction movies. With all their far-fetched plot lines, their improbably moral protagonists, their Earth-shattering stakes. So you can imagine how I felt when I became entangled in one, with no other choice than to help move the story along.

It began with a woman in a ridiculous tiara. She calls herself Rhea, the queen of the Daxamite people. For those unfamiliar with this rather desperate housewife and her ilk, the Daxamites are an alien race without a home. Their planet was destroyed during the same cataclysm that robbed Supergirl of her native world, Krypton.

Unlike the Girl of Steel, however, the Daxamites decided to journey to National City not to become champions for the human race but to conquer them. Rhea even had the unmitigated gall to refer to our planet as New Daxam.

And they would have gotten away with it, too. If not for a ragtag group of freedom fighters led by the aforementioned Supergirl: Green Martians; White Martians; a vigilante calling himself Guardian; two groups of agents from highly classified government installations; the plucky CEO of L-Corp, Lena Luthor; and, of course, the president of the United States. This unlikely band of Saturday-morning misfits teamed together to help save the city from Rhea and dozens of her Daxamite ships, beamed to this world by a matter-transporting device. No easy feat, when one considers that each of Rhea's soldiers possessed abilities paralleling that of Superman. CONTINUED ON FOLLOWING PAGE.

While Cat's writing has always taken a few creative liberties, the gist of her article rings true. Banding together, the heroes of Earth fought off Rhea's forces. Yet despite all our combined efforts, it was Lena and Lillian Luthor who saved the day, using a device from Lex

Luthor's weapons cache that was originally intended to lace the air with kryptonite. They filled the air with a trace amount of lead, an amount harmless to humans, but deadly to Daxamites. The Daxamites had to flee Earth or die.

But that included Mon-El.

Rhea exposed Superman to silver kryptonite, causing Clark to mistake me for his greatest enemy, Zod. I was able to defeat my cousin for the safety of National City, something I never thought even remotely possible before.

I said goodbye to Mon-El today. He couldn't stay here. The air was killing him. I gave him my mother's necklace, and kissed him goodbye.

And I'm not ready to talk about it yet.

Some good came out of the invasion. Alex proposed to Maggie, and Maggie accepted. I'm happy that one of the Danvers sisters got a happy ending.

What I didn't know at the time was that Mon-El's rocket ship was sucked into a wormhole, one that spit him out thousands of years into the future.

Supergirl was honored for my work restoring the city in the wake of the Daxamite invasion. Any other time, all the pomp and circumstance would have been a wonderful reminder of how many people my work touches on a daily basis.

But this time, I wasn't in the mood for celebration. I couldn't think about all the good that we had done. I was stuck obsessing over everything I had lost.

MORGAN EDGE

ALIAS
No known alias

POWERS/ABILITIES
Powerful mogul with high-ranking connections in business, crime, and politics; extremely wealthy, with access to all of Edge Global's vast resources

HOMEWORLD
Earth

WEAKNESSES
Human susceptible to conventional attacks

If you've ever wanted to see what a weasel in a suit looks like, then look no further than Morgan Edge, the corrupt CEO of Edge Global. A real-estate tycoon, Edge would stop at nothing to get his grubby hands on the city's waterfront.

Memo

To: Bloodsport

From: Morgan Edge

Date: June 9

Subject: Waterfront complexes

That's a ridiculous name by the way. But I hear you're a professional, and I am currently in need of a professional's touch.

We have a situation. The city zoning committee is playing hardball, and I'm not a fan of spending more money on bribes than I have to. Therefore, I've decided it's in my best interest to paint the Waterfront as even less of a desirable neighborhood than it currently is. And at the same time, I'd like to start clearing away some of the rabble, prepping the land for my deluxe Waterfront high-rise apartment complexes.

I don't care how you do it. Bomb, missile—hell, get some rogue alien to go on a destructive rampage. Just get it done.

The sooner Edge Global gets its hooks in the Waterfront the better. I don't care if you're "sporting" about it or not.

ALIAS
Robert DuBois

POWERS/ABILITIES
Highly trained ex-military with extensive work in the security field; expert marksman and hand-to-hand combatant; knowledge of Fort Harrison, with probable access to their weapons caches

HOMEWORLD
Earth

WEAKNESSES
Human susceptible to conventional attacks when unprotected

BLOODSPORT

Former military gone AWOL after bombing City Hall, Robert DuBois accepted the identity of a killer for hire, Bloodsport. Employed by Morgan Edge, Bloodsport fired missiles on the Girl of Steel statue unveiling.

So I couldn't help but take the attack personally.

Bloodsport cloaked his submarine by stealing a high-pressure regulator and a Daxamite cloaking device. But he couldn't cloak himself from a Kryptonian's superhearing.

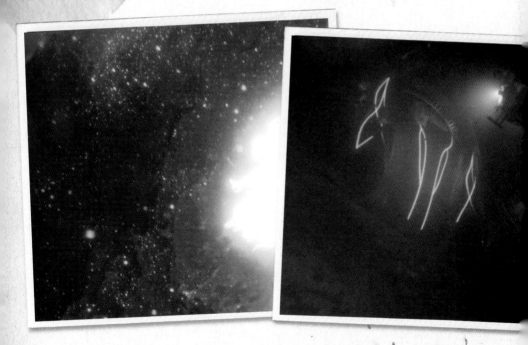

One of Bloodsport's missiles did more than damage the city's bedrock. It dislodged a mysterious spaceship that had been buried for 12,000 years.

The New Face of CatCo

By Kara Danvers

Not all of National City's heroes wear capes.

When she learned that notorious real estate mogul and rumored unscrupulous businessman Morgan Edge was preparing to purchase CatCo Worldwide Media with the intent to slant its coverage in his own political favor, Lena Luthor realized that she had to act. As the chairwoman and CEO of L-Corp, Luthor is not a stranger to corporate politics. And since Luthor is a fan of CatCo, this was one backroom deal she planned on interrupting.

"CatCo has stood for integrity ever since Cat Grant founded it

When Mon-El left, things were pretty rocky for me at first. I threw myself into being Supergirl, and even quit my job at CatCo. Luckily for Kara Danvers, when Lena Luthor bought CatCo to make sure Morgan Edge couldn't use the paper for his own nefarious propaganda, she convinced me to reclaim the reporter job I had worked so hard for.

years ago," says Luthor. "They have presented fair and balanced coverage of current events since Grant's original acquisition of the *National City Tribune*, and have kept that tradition alive, through the leadership of James Olsen and Snapper Carr."

While the aforementioned Carr is currently on an extended sabbatical from *CatCo* magazine, Olsen is still very much serving as the head of CatCo Worldwide Media. He was as shocked as anyone when Luthor stepped in, seemingly out of nowhere, and purchased CatCo from under Edge's nose, taking a hands-on approach with the company and installing newcomer Samantha Arias as CFO of L-Corp to run that corporation's day-to-day operations.

"No one was more surprised than me," says Olsen. "I've seen plenty of power moves in my days in a newsroom, but Lena's topped them all."

Officially taking over the business Thursday, Luthor has no intention of changing the many well-oiled machines housed under the CatCo Worldwide Media banner. "If it's working, why change it?" Luthor says.

National City citizens can rest assured that *CatCo* magazine will continue the same journalistic integrity that built it into the institution it is today. Sometimes it takes more than a Supergirl to save the day. Sometimes it takes a Luthor.

When Lena took control of her company, Cat Grant didn't seem to mind in the least. She had moved on to her new career as a press secretary for President Marsdin, applying that old Cat Grant "charm" on the entire nation.

KING NEWS

RESS SECRETARY CAT G

BREAKING NEWS

BREAKING NEWS

An excerpt from the journal of Samantha Arias. If only Sam had listened to her daughter. Maybe things could have been different.

Things have gotten out of hand with Ruby. This . . . superhero obsession of hers has gone way too far. Ever since I lifted that fallen tower off her at the statue unveiling ceremony, she's been different. Too different.

First it was the fight at school with Stephanie Harrison, when Ruby claimed I had superpowers and punched Stephanie when she didn't believe her.

Then she purposely put herself in harm's way during that attack by that metahuman woman, whoever she was. She actually walked headfirst into danger, into the path of an out-of-control wrecking ball, just to force me to save her life. If Supergirl hadn't been there, I wouldn't be writing this journal entry right now. I wouldn't be doing anything.

No matter what I say or do, Ruby seems convinced that I have enhanced abilities. But that's impossible. I know it's just the runaway imagination of a little girl, but . . . but if I know that, then why am I trying to bend crowbars when no one's looking? All adrenaline aside, how did I lift that tower?

I feel crazy for even writing any of this. I start tomorrow as the CFO of L-Corp, and this entry is proof positive I'm truly in need of a good night's sleep.

ALIAS
Gayle Marsh

POWERS/ABILITIES
Extremely powerful psionic and psychic abilities; can infiltrate the minds of others and unlock their deepest fears

HOMEWORLD
Earth

WEAKNESSES
Powers can be overridden by strength of mind and the pure will of her targeted victims

PSI

She calls herself Psi, a metahuman who can out-psychic the Martian Manhunter himself. When we first fought, Psi was able to use my own fears against me, making me see my mother and relive my escape from Krypton.

PSIONIC INHIBITOR RAY

OKAY, SO IF I'VE GOT THIS THING TUNED CORRECTLY—AND THERE'S A CHANCE THAT I DON'T—ALL SUPERGIRL HAS TO DO IS GET CLOSE ENOUGH TO PSI TO ACTIVATE THE INHIBITOR RAY. BEST CASE SCENARIO, PSI'S POWERS GET REDUCED TO THE LEVEL OF A PSYCHIC HELP LINE. WORST CASE? BETTER OFF NOT TALKING ABOUT THAT.

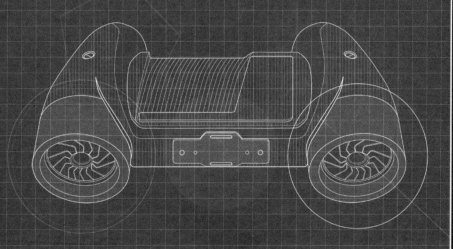

Not one of Winn's best designs. When I first saw the inhibitor ray, I thought it looked like an old-fashioned Earth telephone that lit up. Now that I think about it, it really might have been just that. For all the good it did me, at least . . .

I was only able to beat Psi when I overcame my own fear. It wasn't easy, but people don't just go around calling me Supergirl for nothing.

While he didn't ask for help, when J'onn received a distress call from M'gann on Mars, I made sure I was right there with him, flying back to his homeworld in one of the coolest rides I've ever seen.

CH'EVRO'LAY
PASSENGER CAR
SPACECRAFT HYBRID

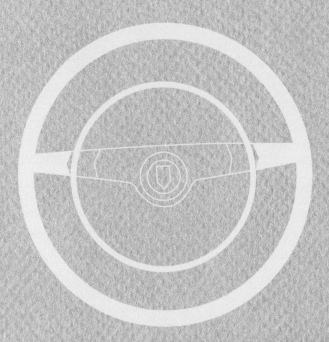

SHOP MANUAL

1949-53 MODELS
INCLUDES 1954 SUPPLEMENT

RS-34-MM

J'onn J'onzz comes from a race of shapeshifters. I guess it only makes sense that their technology shape-shifts, too.

When we arrived on Mars, J'onn was shocked to discover that his father, M'yrnn, was still alive. It took some convincing, but eventually M'yrnn realized that J'onn was indeed his son, and not simply the product of some White Martian trick.

Our ride home was certainly a happier one, as I shared the car with two Green Martians, eager to start a new life together on Earth.

Oh, the sights I have seen!

My son swears I will get used to it, but how can one become accustomed to such a vibrant world? The grass of the place they call the park is so green. The leaves on the trees are so full of life! Even in its heyday, Mars was never such an oasis.

The humans, they bury these marvels under concrete walkways and monuments to their businessmen, but I find those giant steel constructions no less remarkable. J'onn says the buildings are full of office workers. I envy these officers very much. I have heard that a secretary is quite a touted position, given governance over the very means of communication. I think this shall be my career path of choice if opportunity so presents itself.

And the cuisine! I can't believe I have written this many English characters and have not yet mentioned the delicacies that Earth has to offer the palate! Why just today, I consumed a metal tube of Soder Cola, a beverage that not only quenches one's thirst, but also adds a playful touch of carbonation to delight and rouse the interest of the tongue and throat. Tomorrow, I shall return to the store called the Bo'Dega and purchase the diet variation of this delicious drink. I do not know what "diet" tastes like, but I'm sure it will be an absolute thrill for the senses!

Oh, life! Oh, marvelous Earth!

A page from M'yrnn's journal. J'onn says it's an improvement over his previous entry, when M'yrnn used the pages of J'onn's favorite book, *Moby-Dick*, to write a lengthy dissertation about tasting Chocos cookies for the first time.

In an effort to bond with his father, J'onn eventually found an apartment for both of them to share. I have a feeling that the personal lives of those two are like some early '90s sitcom.

ALIAS
No known alias

POWERS/ABILITIES
Extensive knowledge of Kryptonian history; charismatic and persuasive leader

HOMEWORLD
Earth

WEAKNESSES
Human susceptible to conventional attacks

THOMAS COVILLE

Thomas Coville became obsessed with all things Kryptonian after I saved him and the rest of Flight 237. He began buying up anything Kryptonian he could get his hands on, and even started his own cult dedicated to the Kryptonian sun god, Rao.

JOIN US.

Thomas was convinced there were three steps for the coming "end of days": the Mark of the Beast, the Work of the Beast, and the Reign of the Beast. I was convinced that he was completely insane when he tried to show his faith in Supergirl by bombing a sporting arena.

I think the truth was somewhere in the middle.

When reports of children suffering from lead poisoning began to become public knowledge, Morgan Edge was quick to point the finger at Lena Luthor and her use of lead to ward off the Daxamite invasion.

As it turned out, Edge himself was using one of his subsidiary companies to poison a local swimming pool in an attempt to frame Lena.

ACRE LEE CHEMICALS
A SUBSIDIARY OF EDGE GLOBAL
Safe Ethical Science for a World of Results

"Ethical" and "Edge" are two words that do not go together under any circumstance.

In a page out of her brother's handbook, Lena took matters into her own hands. She would have murdered Edge had one of his lackeys not sucker-punched her from behind. He then placed her on a plane loaded with the same Acre Lee chemicals, headed for the city's water supply.

I was able to save both Lena and the cargo, but once again, Edge covered his tracks, making it impossible to pin the crime on him. I don't condone what Lena tried to do to Edge, but I can certainly understand it.

ALIAS
Imra Ardeen

POWERS/ABILITIES
Advanced telekinesis; possesses Legion flight ring that allows flight; extensive knowledge of the future; trained in Legion protocol and hand-to-hand combat techniques

HOMEWORLD
Titan

WEAKNESSES
Can be susceptible to conventional attacks when her mind is distracted or unguarded

SATURN GIRL

I honestly don't even know where to begin. Mon-El is back. He's here on Earth and he can breathe the air and he looks the same and I should be ecstatic. But I'm not. Because despite everything I just wrote, Mon-El is most definitely not the same.

While he was only gone seven months to me, Mon-El was pulled into the future thanks to a wormhole in space. He was in the 31st century, living life and forming a group of heroes called the Legion. I have a hard enough time wrapping my head around the time travel stuff, let alone the idea of a Mon-El organized and motivated enough to found a superhero team. And while I moped around my apartment, he returned here, trapped in suspended animation for 12,000 years in the Legion Cruiser until Bloodsport's attack damaged his ship and set him free.

But none of that time, none of that distance, explains the weird look in his eyes when we talk. The way his smile is just slightly off. No, that only made sense when he finally admitted to me that while he was away, he had married Imra Ardeen, a fellow Legionnaire.

So that's it. My boyfriend is married to someone else. And I don't know whether to cry, scream, or punch a hole in a planet.

MON-EL DISAPPEARS, AND THEN THIS MON-EL ARRIVES WITH FACIAL HAIR? THAT'S A SURE SIGN OF AN EVIL DOPPELGÄNGER, RIGHT THERE. IT'S SCI-FI 101, PEOPLE! —WINN

OVERGIRL

ALIAS
Kara Zor-El

POWERS/ABILITIES
Super-strength, endurance, speed, agility, and durability; heat, microscopic, x-ray, and telescopic vision; accelerated healing; freeze breath; flight

HOMEWORLD
Krypton-X

WEAKNESSES
Kryptonite, red sun radiation, magic manipulation

When the Flash and his longtime girlfriend, Iris West, finally decided to get married, I was honored to sing at their wedding. Sure, I was going through a lot of personal stuff, but seeing those two together would put a smile on anyone's face.

Except, apparently, Nazis. Yeah, so Barry's wedding was crashed by Nazis from Earth-X.

Kindly Reply

KARA DANVERS & MON-EL

—— ACCEPTS WITH PLEASURE

—— DECLINES WITH REGRETS

PLEASE INDICATE ENTRÉE CHOICE

BEEF   CHICKEN   VEGETARIAN

Always great to see your ex's name on the RSVP. Needless to say, I decided to bring Alex instead.

Alex and Maggie had broken off their engagement when they couldn't reconcile their plans for the future. Alex wanted kids, Maggie firmly did not. So Alex used the wedding as an excuse to find a rebound fling in the form of White Canary.

There are very few things in this world as disturbing as meeting your Nazi doppelgänger from a parallel dimension. Mine was called Overgirl. She was dying, and her only chance at life was to steal my heart and transfer it to her body.

Thanks to the help of nearly every superhero on Earth-1, Overgirl and her husband, Earth-X's Green Arrow (totally not my type, by the way), weren't able to secure my heart. Without the transplant, Overgirl went supernova. The Nazis were defeated, and from what I've heard, Barry and Iris married each other during a private ceremony alongside Green Arrow and Overwatch (still love her, btw), who tied the knot at the same time.

When Krypton exploded, I wasn't the only girl who was sent to Earth in a small rocket ship. A dark cult sent a baby girl to Earth, a being augmented to bring death and destruction. She was programmed to be a World Killer. To Reign.

ALIAS
Samantha Arias

POWERS/ABILITIES
Super-strength, endurance, speed, agility, and durability; heat, microscopic, x-ray, and telescopic vision; accelerated healing; freeze breath; flight

HOMEWORLD
Krypton

WEAKNESSES
Magic manipulation; rational appeals to civilian identity/alternate personality

REIGN

I first fought the masked villain called Reign after she began carving her symbol all over National City. To draw her out of the shadows, I burned the symbol of the House of El onto the top of the CatCo building. It worked faster than I expected.

She was as strong as me, if not stronger. Worse, she was more determined than me, ready to win no matter the cost.

What I didn't know at the time was that Reign was actually a new friend of mine. L-Corp's CFO, Samantha Arias.

Samantha's investigation into her past led her to her own Kryptonian headquarters on Earth, the Fortress of Sanctuary.

Sam's adoptive mother, Patricia, hid her rocket ship from her, as well as her Kryptonian heritage.

If I was surprised to find out that Sam and Reign were one and the same, imagine Sam's shock.

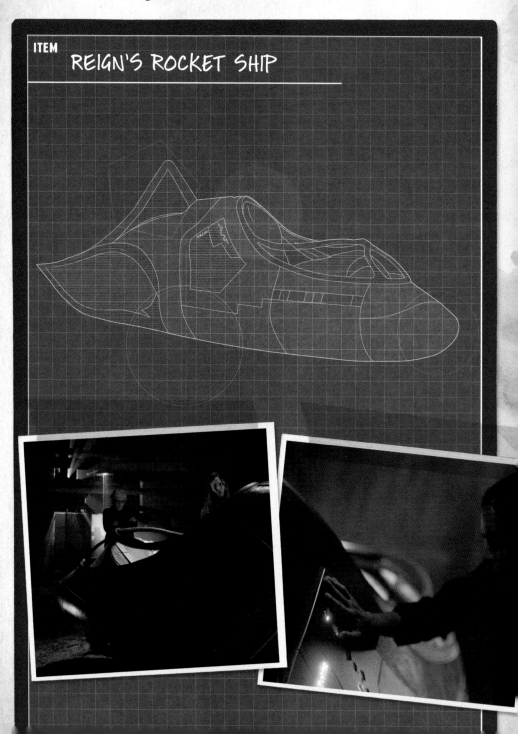

ITEM

REIGN'S ROCKET SHIP

When Reign and I first fought, I was no match for her precision and determination. After the most brutal battle of my life, she dropped me off a building, successfully landing me in a coma.

Memo

The Department of Extranormal Operations: Confidential

Request for materials:

In order for the Sundown Protocol to function at optimal levels, ensuring success if faced with a rogue Kryptonian or a mind-altered Superman or Supergirl, we are requesting the following additional items for next year's inventory:

Kryptonite Darts (8 lbs. of kryptonite total)
Red Sun Grenades (48)
Sonic Grenades (48)

These are the bare-minimum supplies needed to better arm the task force above standard DEO weaponry.

—Agent Vasquez

The DEO had a contingency plan for rogue Kryptonians. Called the Sundown Protocol, it was completely ineffective on Reign. Reign seemed to have all my powers, yet none of my weaknesses.

ALIAS
Querl Dox

POWERS/ABILITIES
12th-level intellect; expert at controlling future technology; possesses Legion flight ring that allows flight; extensive knowledge of the future; trained in Legion protocol and hand-to-hand combat techniques

HOMEWORLD
Colu

WEAKNESSES
Susceptible to conventional attacks when unprepared

BRAINIAC 5

A future member of the Brainiac lineage, making him related to Indigo, Brainiac 5 is using his 12th-level intellect to try to bring honor to the Brainiac name. One corrupt aunt seems like nothing compared to the family history Brainy has to deal with.

Dear Diary,

Well, that was a weird couple of days. When you wake up in your apartment after a lazy nap, the last thing you expect to discover is a blue alien from the future at your front door. The second-to-last thing you expect to find out is that this isn't your apartment at all, but a construct of a safe space created by your mind as you rest in a coma aboard a 31st-century spacecraft's stasis tank.

That's what happened to me. After Reign thoroughly trounced me, it took the combined efforts of Legion member Brainiac 5 and my own willpower to escape the comfy trap my own brain built for me. I thought escaping the Black Mercy's dream world was tough. It was even harder figuring out the puzzle I had set for myself.

In the end, I had to realize that Kara Danvers was the one who needed to escape the prison of my mind, not Supergirl. Kara is the real me. My sister's favorite person. My best self. Once I realized that, it was a simple matter of getting up and walking out my apartment door.

The Legion of Super-Heroes

The idea that this team of superheroes from the future is inspired by my actions . . . it's overwhelming.

It's also frustrating, as the Legion members couldn't really give us any information about our time, like clues for helping us defeat Reign. In 2455, Earth experienced a third-degree extinction phenomenon. This meant they had no records about the 21st century aside from the main bullet points.

Okay, so I'm just now getting the hang of reading Interlac. Next up, Saturnian . . .

I know I can naturally fly on Earth, but I wouldn't say no to my own Legion Flight Ring. Maybe if I compliment Brainiac's enough, he'll get the hint. He is supposed to be super smart . . .

L-Corp apparently develops a cure for the lead poisoning in the atmosphere in the near future, making it possible for Mon-El to breathe in our time. What Mon-El and I didn't know, however, was that the Legion had a hidden agenda for coming to the 21st century.

In an effort to find out more about Reign, I decided to head to Fort Rozz to locate Priestess Jindah Kol Rozz. The only problem was, Fort Rozz was currently revolving around a blue star, a sun fatal to men, and one where I'd be without powers. If I hoped to survive, I'd need a team of the toughest women any universe had to offer.

Possible Candidates for the Fort Rozz Mission:

- ~~Miss Martian~~ – too busy with the Mars revolution.
- ~~Alex~~ – she's got enough going on in her life right now.
- Imra – not particularly excited about this choice, but it makes logical sense. (Keep it professional, Kara.)
- Livewire – okay, so she might zap me or kill me or something, but I've seen through her tough-girl act before. I think there might be some good under all that static.
- Psi – same deal as Livewire (although way more of a chance that she'll kill me).
- ~~Vixen~~ – so she hails from another Earth and might be in another time period. Her powers are so cool!
- ~~J'onn~~ – can't he just shape-shift into a woman or something?
- ~~Cat Grant~~ – nothing can kill this lady. Who better to sign up for a suicide mission?

We finally discovered Jindah Kol Rozz, but the priestess wasn't much help. She did mention two other World Killers besides Reign: beings called Purity and Pestilence.

Livewire sacrificed herself to save my life. She'd hate me for calling her a hero, but that's exactly what she was in the end.

One of the straggling items stolen from Lex Luthor's weapons cache came back to haunt us when Lillian Luthor attacked Morgan Edge at Edge's own party. Knowing that Edge had attempted to murder her daughter, Lillian apparently decided to take action.

This is her idea of helping.

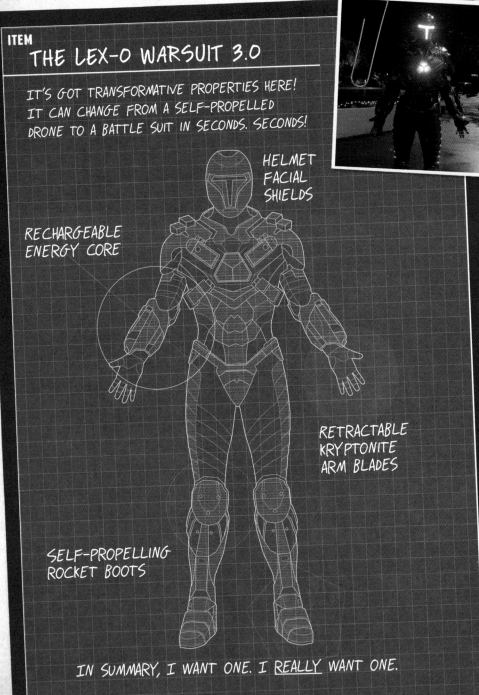

ITEM

THE LEX-O WARSUIT 3.0

IT'S GOT TRANSFORMATIVE PROPERTIES HERE!
IT CAN CHANGE FROM A SELF-PROPELLED
DRONE TO A BATTLE SUIT IN SECONDS. SECONDS!

HELMET
FACIAL
SHIELDS

RECHARGEABLE
ENERGY CORE

RETRACTABLE
KRYPTONITE
ARM BLADES

SELF-PROPELLING
ROCKET BOOTS

IN SUMMARY, I WANT ONE. I <u>REALLY</u> WANT ONE.

During the chaos of the attack, Lena was able to get a taped confession out of Morgan Edge admitting to a failed attempt at having her killed. Lillian was apprehended by the authorities, but whether a slippery snake like Edge will ever see the inside of a jail cell remains to be seen.

After Priestess Rozz revealed there were two other World Killers besides Reign, the DEO began to furiously search for them. We discovered that they weren't strictly Kryptonian, but that they were augmented, genetically altered to be immune to my weaknesses.

ALIAS
Julia Freeman

POWERS/ABILITIES
Sonic projection from Kryptonian modification; super-strength, endurance, speed, agility, and durability; assumed heat, microscopic, x-ray, and telescopic vision; accelerated healing; freeze breath; flight

HOMEWORLD
Krypton

WEAKNESSES
Rational appeals to civilian identity/alternate personality; sonic dampeners can counteract her sonic abilities

PURITY

When we found Julia, she was snapping in and out of her Purity identity. She was battling her programming, and, if not for Reign's interruption, I truly think we would have gotten through to her.

We don't need to fight these women. We need to save them.

ALIAS

Dr. Grace Parker, Blight (in the 31st century)

POWERS/ABILITIES

Able to spread disease with a scratch of her fingernails; super-strength, endurance, speed, agility, and durability; assumed heat, microscopic, x-ray, and telescopic vision; accelerated healing; freeze breath; flight

HOMEWORLD

Krypton

WEAKNESSES

Susceptible to attacks from fellow Kryptonians, including Purity

PESTILENCE

Pestilence was not just another World Killer. She was destined to become Blight, a devastating force of nature in the 31st century. She was the true reason that the Legion had come back to our time in the first place, but she was killed when Purity turned on her.

So that's my story. Of course, it isn't over. No matter how many times I put on the S and the red cape, no matter how many fires I put out or alien invasions I ward off, there always seems to be more I can do, more people I can help.

And honestly, I wouldn't have it any other way. I'm here on Earth for a reason. Just like my cousin, I'm here to protect those who need it. To fight for those who can't fight for themselves. To serve as a symbol of light to those who have lost all hope.

You've read my secrets. You've seen the demons I've fought, and those I've yet to overcome. And now you're a part of it. You're part of something greater than yourself. Greater than me. Greater than National City.

So put your head down, ball up your fists, and join me on the battlefield in whatever way you can. Because it takes more than just one Supergirl to make this world a better place.

Episode Guide

Season 1

Episode 1: "Pilot"

As the planet Krypton is about to explode, a young girl named Kara Zor-El is sent to Earth in a rocket ship. Her mission was to protect her baby cousin, Kal-El, but her rocket gets caught in the otherworldly Phantom Zone for twenty-four years before eventually breaching that dimension and landing on Earth. With Kal-El now a full-grown man and a superhero due to enhanced abilities from the radiation of Earth's yellow sun, Kara is sent to live with the Danvers family, and grows up alongside her sister, Alex. Years later, Kara is an employee at CatCo Worldwide Media in National City as the personal assistant to CEO Cat Grant. When her sister is trapped onboard an airplane with engine failure, Kara uses her abilities publicly to save the plane. She reveals her secret to coworker Winn Schott Jr., who designs a costume for her. Kara is dubbed Supergirl by Cat Grant. Kara is soon kidnapped by the Department of Extranormal Operations, a secret government organization charged with protecting Earth from alien threats, where she learns her sister, Alex, has been working with them for years. Supergirl stops an alien named Vartox, who secretly works for Kara's Kryptonian aunt, Astra, and is just one of the many villains who escaped from the Phantom Zone at the same time as Kara's rocket ship. Afterward, Kara decides to team with the DEO on a regular basis, but yet had one more surprise waiting for her. Her love interest at CatCo, new employee James Olsen, reveals he knows her secret identity and was sent from Metropolis by Superman to keep an eye on Kal-El's now "younger" cousin.

Episode 2: "Stronger Together"

Supergirl begins to train with the DEO and its director, Hank Henshaw. However, things take a deadly turn when a Hellgrammite alien kidnaps Alex and brings her to Astra to set a trap for Supergirl. Kara fights her aunt while Alex kills the Hellgrammite with his own stinger, but the battle ends abruptly when Astra is injured by a kryptonite knife wielded by Henshaw. Back at CatCo, Supergirl agrees to be interviewed by Cat Grant to help relieve pressures put on James Olsen, who was tasked with nabbing an exclusive with Supergirl.

Episode 3: "Fight or Flight"

Supergirl is interviewed by Cat and accidentally reveals that she's Superman's cousin. This inspires former Superman villain Reactron to attempt to get his revenge on the Man of Steel by killing Supergirl. During their fight, Supergirl damages Reactron's suit, causing the villain to abduct Lord Technologies' CEO Maxwell Lord to repair it. While Supergirl is rescued by Superman during her next battle with Reactron, she successfully removes the power core in Reactron's suit during their final fight, defeating the criminal. In her private life, Kara's feelings for James become a bit more complicated when his ex-girlfriend, Lucy Lane, arrives in National City.

Episode 4: "Livewire"

Kara hosts a Thanksgiving dinner for her foster mother, Eliza, and Alex and Winn. However, a family squabble erupts, and Alex admits to working at the DEO, the department that used to employ her father, Jeremiah, before his untimely death during a mission. Meanwhile, shock jock turned metahuman Livewire attempts to murder the boss who scorned her, Cat Grant. Supergirl finally stops her by spraying her with water.

Episode 5: "How Does She Do It?"

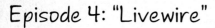

Kara is charged with babysitting Cat's son, Carter, but the boy gets away from her in order to attend Max Lord's new super train launch. When a bomber tries to blow up the train, Supergirl stops him and saves Carter, yet the bomber dies in the process. Suspicious of the event, Supergirl discovers that Lord himself was behind the bombing, having staged the entire situation to test Supergirl's limits and abilities.

Episode 6: "Red Faced"

Supergirl is confronted by General Sam Lane and his daughter, Major Lucy Lane, when they want to test Supergirl's powers against their android, Red Tornado. Supergirl beats the robot but is soon forced to battle it again when its rogue inventor, T. O. Morrow, forces the android to attack General Lane. Alex confronts and kills Morrow, leaving Supergirl to dispatch his out-of-control robot. To defeat the powerful creation, Supergirl expends much of her solar energy, temporarily losing her powers as a result.

Episode 7: "Human for a Day"

An earthquake strikes National City at the absolute worst time: the day when Supergirl has lost her powers. When James Olsen nearly dies in the elevator shaft at CatCo, Supergirl's adrenaline spikes and she regains her powers just in time to rescue him. Back at the DEO, the earthquake allows a powerful alien named Jemm to escape. Hank Henshaw defeats Jemm in front of Alex, revealing that he is in fact named J'onn J'onzz, the Martian Manhunter. When the real Hank Henshaw seemingly killed Jeremiah Danvers some time ago and then died himself, J'onn took Hank's place as the head of the DEO.

Episode 8: "Hostile Takeover"

Attacked by Astra in the previous episode, Supergirl eventually overpowers her aunt and imprisons her at the DEO. However, her capture was merely a distraction that allowed Astra's husband, Non, to attack Lord Technologies. Meanwhile, at CatCo, Kara helps Cat discover a board member who had been leaking her personal information, but in the process, Kara discovers that Cat has a secret son named Adam Foster. Cat also reveals that she knows that Supergirl and Kara are one and the same.

Episode 9: "Blood Bonds"

Non manages to escape Supergirl's clutches and kidnaps Martian Manhunter. He tries to trade J'onn for Astra but is rejected by General Sam Lane. After Lane walks into a trap set by Astra, Supergirl and Alex ignore his objections and make the trade. The rescued J'onn then takes the form of Supergirl and appears in front of Cat Grant alongside Kara to throw off any suspicions Cat may have about her assistant's private life.

Episode 10: "Childish Things"

Winn's father is revealed to be Superman's old foe the Toyman when the villain breaks out of prison and contacts his son. Toyman soon forces Winn to attempt to murder the man who stole the Toyman's designs years earlier, Chester Dunholtz. Supergirl interrupts and saves the day. Meanwhile, Lucy Lane takes a new job as Cat Grant's lawyer, Winn reveals his feelings for Kara, and J'onn infiltrates Maxwell Lord's lab to find a comatose test subject. Nearly always smarter than his adversaries, Lord discovers that Supergirl and Alex are sisters.

Episode 11: "Strange Visitor from Another Planet"

J'onn takes things personally when a White Martian rears its ugly head in National City in an attempt to murder Senator Miranda Crane. After revealing to his DEO allies that White Martians killed off the Green Martian race, J'onn trades himself for the captive Alex Danvers, and Supergirl intervenes, resulting in the White Martian's capture. Back at CatCo, Kara helps Cat Grant reconcile with her son Adam and is unexpectedly asked out on a date by the young man.

Episode 12: "Bizarro"

Supergirl discovers that Maxwell Lord's test subject is her exact double bent on destroying the real Supergirl. Hunting down Kara while she's on her date with Adam, this "Bizarro" Supergirl's face becomes chalky and bizarre when the DEO exposes her to kryptonite. After breaking things off with Adam, Supergirl faces Bizarro when the villain kidnaps James Olsen. Alex shoots Bizarro with a modified blue kryptonite, and the unwitting villain is taken into custody. Meanwhile, the mastermind behind Bizarro, Maxwell Lord, is locked in a DEO holding cell.

Episode 13: "For the Girl Who Has Everything"

Supergirl experiences a near-perfect dream world in her mind when she falls prey to an alien Black Mercy plant delivered to her by Non. With the Martian Manhunter's help, Alex enters Kara's fantasy of an ideal Krypton to talk her back to reality. Now safely back in the real world, an enraged Kara attacks Non while Alex and J'onn battle Astra. During the course of the battle, Alex impales Astra on a kryptonite blade, killing her. J'onn takes the blame for the death to keep goodwill between the Danvers sisters.

Episode 14: "Truth, Justice, and the American Way"

Supergirl and Non declare a cease-fire so they can mourn Astra's death, during which Supergirl and her DEO allies hunt down an armored alien called the Master Jailer, a former guard from the Phantom Zone's prison, Fort Rozz. Killing alien fugitives no matter their crimes, the Master Jailer captures Supergirl but the heroine escapes his clutches and defeats him before he can execute her. Back at the DEO, it is decided to free Maxwell Lord when CatCo begins to become curious about his disappearance. While at CatCo, Cat Grant hires a new assistant, Siobhan Smythe, to force a competition with Kara.

Episode 15: "Solitude"

An alien hacker named Indigo attempts to deliver illegally gained information to Cat Grant, but Cat refuses the data on principle. Indigo's true intention is to destroy National City by breaking into a nuclear base's missile launching system. Supergirl stops the missile while Winn uploads a virus to Indigo. Indigo is seemingly destroyed, but only after she reveals that she was the one who dislodged Kara's rocket ship from the Phantom Zone all those years ago, linking it to Fort Rozz in the process. She is later revived by Non. Meanwhile, the personal lives of Kara's friends seem more chaotic than usual. James and Lucy break up, Winn begins dating Siobhan, and Alex reveals to Kara that she was the one who killed Astra, but she quickly earns her sister's forgiveness.

Episode 16: "Falling"

A crueler side of Supergirl is revealed when she is unexpectedly exposed to red kryptonite while on patrol. As Kara Danvers, she takes steps to expose Siobhan's double dealings, causing Smythe to be fired. As Supergirl, she drops Cat from a building, nearly killing her. Cat takes to the airways to denounce the hero she once so proudly touted. The creator of the red kryptonite, Maxwell Lord, is forced to join forces with Alex Danvers to stop and cure Supergirl. While they are successful at the attempt and return Supergirl back to normal, the Martian Manhunter's double identity is outed in the process.

Episode 17: "Manhunter"

Colonel James Harper and a reenlisted Major Lucy Lane dig into Martian Manhunter's past while investigating him for the government. When Harper decides to ship J'onn and Alex to the corrupt institution called Project Cadmus, Supergirl reveals her identity to Lucy to plead for her help. They successfully help Alex and J'onn escape, who set out to find Jeremiah Danvers when they learn he's still alive. Lucy is later promoted to the head of the DEO.

Episode 18: "World's Finest"

Discovering her family has a history of the curse of the banshee, Siobhan uses her newly discovered sonic scream to strike out at those who she believes wronged her, namely Kara Danvers. As the villain Silver Banshee, Siobhan frees Livewire and partners with the electrical villain to kill both Kara and Cat Grant. However, when the Flash speeds into National City, Supergirl gains a partner in crime-fighting to help defeat the villains before the hero runs back to his own dimension of Earth-1.

Episode 19: "Myriad"

Non's ultimate plot is revealed when the citizens of National City become his mindless puppets due to the Kryptonian Myriad weapon. Maxwell Lord and Cat Grant are unaffected due to Lord's technology and the earrings he had gifted Cat with previously. While Superman is under Non's influence, Supergirl's mind remains her own. However, after Indigo bests the Martian Manhunter and Alex, Non uses Myriad to force Alex and Supergirl to battle each other to the death.

Episode 20: "Better Angels"

A mind-controlled Alex battles her sister and nearly kills her with the kryptonite sword she used to kill Astra. However, Eliza snaps her daughter back to reality just in time, giving Supergirl the chance to broadcast a hopeful message to the citizens of National City and break Myriad's hold on them. Non and Indigo decide to increase the Myriad frequency to kill all the humans on Earth. Supergirl and Martian Manhunter face off with the two villains outside Fort Rozz and prevail. Supergirl then flies Fort Rozz into space so that Myriad can no longer harm anyone. When the smoke clears, J'onn is reinstated as the head of the DEO, and Kara is given a promotion at CatCo. Despite the frantic pace of her recent life, Supergirl isn't prepared for her next major shock: a Kryptonian rocket ship crash-landing nearby.

Season 2

Episode 1: "The Adventures of Supergirl"

After discovering an adult man inside the crashed Kryptonian rocket ship, Supergirl saves an American spacecraft suffering from engine failure with the help of her cousin, Superman. The two soon learn that the new CEO of Luthor Corp, Lena Luthor, is in danger. During a ceremony where she renames her company L-Corp to distance it from her corrupt half-brother, Lex Luthor, Lena is targeted by an assassin named John Corben, a criminal who is eventually shot by Lena herself. In her personal life, Kara decides not to pursue her budding romantic relationship with James, and focuses on her new promotion as a reporter at CatCo. Winn takes a job at the DEO, and Corben is taken to Project Cadmus, where he is given a new lease on life as the villain Metallo.

Episode 2: "The Last Children of Krypton"

Superman decides to stick around National City and spend some time with his cousin. However, things turn deadly for the pair when Corben returns as Metallo, powered by a kryptonite heart and partnered with a fellow cyborg. Using anti-kryptonite armor designed by Winn, Superman and Supergirl defeat the Metallos. Superman returns to Metropolis after the Martian Manhunter gives him the DEO's supply of kryptonite, burying an old wound between the two heroes. Back at CatCo, Kara meets her new boss, Snapper Carr, whom she clashes with immediately. However, Kara doesn't receive support from Cat Grant, as Cat announces a leave of absence from her company, placing James Olsen in charge.

Episode 3: "Welcome to Earth"

President Marsdin arrives in National City to sign an act that will give aliens amnesty. However, her mission of intergalactic goodwill is interrupted when she's attacked by a would-be assassin, whom the DEO mistakenly believes to be the escaped man Supergirl discovered in the Kryptonian rocket ship. The attacker is soon revealed to be the villain Scorcher, but Supergirl and her DEO allies manage to stop her. With the rocket ship refugee back in custody and revealed to be a Daxamite, Supergirl looks past the age-old prejudices and animosity between Kryptonians and the Daxamite people and releases the alien man, who is revealed to be named Mon-El. Supergirl also reveals to him that Daxam was destroyed at the same time as Krypton. Meanwhile, Kara interviews Lena Luthor and is skeptical of the alien detection device Lena's people have developed, and at an alien dive bar, the Martian Manhunter meets a bartender named M'gann M'orzz, who he soon believes to be a fellow surviving Green Martian.

Episode 4: "Survivors"

When the criminal Roulette is discovered to host alien death bouts for the entertainment of her rich clientele, Supergirl interrupts the festivities and is forced to battle the alien warrior Draaga. While Roulette escapes the encounter, the Martian Manhunter notices M'gann is one of the fighters and confronts her. M'gann then sets J'onn up to be kidnapped by Roulette. With Roulette's bouts moved to a new location, Kara secures an invitation to the fights from Lena Luthor, but not before J'onn and M'gann are forced to fight one another. J'onn talks some sense into his fellow Martian, and when Supergirl arrives to defeat Draaga in a rematch, Roulette is taken into custody, albeit briefly. Despite M'gann's apparent change in allegiance, neither Supergirl nor the Martian Manhunter know that she is secretly a White Martian in disguise.

Episode 5: "Crossfire"

Lena's mother, Lillian Luthor, is revealed to be the mastermind behind Cadmus, the clandestine organization that hires criminals to terrorize National City using alien weaponry. Back at CatCo, Mon-El gets a job as an intern named Mike, but can't seem to adapt to Earth's social graces, prompting Alex to advise Kara to let Mon-El find his own path as a civilian. When his dad's prized camera is broken, James Olsen opts to become a vigilante and attempts to convince Winn to help him.

Episode 6: "Changing"

A scientist named Rudy Jones is infected with an alien parasite and begins to murder others. Supergirl and the Martian Manhunter confront him, but their powers are partially drained. J'onn is injured enough that he requires a blood transfusion from M'gann. Supergirl recovers and finds the Parasite again, fighting him with the help of James in his new identity as the Guardian. The Parasite is bested when Supergirl causes him to absorb Plutonium 239. Meanwhile, Alex develops feelings for police officer Maggie Sawyer but is rejected, and Mon-El is abducted by Cadmus.

Episode 7: "The Darkest Place"

Supergirl visits Cadmus and encounters the real Hank Henshaw, now called the Cyborg Superman. Forced to expel enough solar flare through her heat vision to deplete her powers and therefore allow Lillian Luthor to take a blood sample from her, Supergirl eventually escapes with Mon-El in tow, thanks to the help of the very much alive Jeremiah Danvers. Meanwhile, the Guardian tracks down a serial killer, earning Supergirl's trust.

Episode 8: "Medusa"

Cyborg Superman gases the alien dive bar, killing many of its patrons. Visiting Superman's Fortress of Solitude, Supergirl learns that Cyborg Superman was planning on using the Kryptonian virus called Medusa to kill aliens on Earth. Lena Luthor gives her mother the isotope necessary to disperse Medusa but in reality switches it out to make the virus inert. Lillian is arrested, but Cyborg Superman eludes capture. Just when things seemed to have calmed down a bit, the Flash from Earth-1 arrives again, requesting Supergirl's help against an alien invasion. Supergirl volunteers her assistance, fighting the invading Dominator hordes in *The Flash*, Season 3, Episode 8; *Arrow*, Season 5, Episode 8; and *Legends of Tomorrow*, Season 2, Episode 7.

Episode 9: "Supergirl Lives"

Supergirl and Mon-El track a few missing persons to a faux clinical trial operation that has been using humans as slaves on the planet Maaldoria. Without their powers due to the red sun Maaldoria orbits, Supergirl and Mon-El are captured, discovering that Roulette is among the slave traders. While Winn has been doubting himself because he was injured while assisting the Guardian, he proves himself when he and Alex successfully rescue Supergirl, Mon-El, and the slaves.

Episode 10: "We Can Be Heroes"

Supergirl, Mon-El, and the Guardian find themselves up against two new villains who use Livewire's powers against the heroes. The group soon discovers that a scientist has been siphoning off Livewire's abilities and giving them to his test subjects as they hold the supervillain hostage. Supergirl locates and frees Livewire, trading the villain her freedom to spare the life of the corrupt scientist. In addition, Martian Manhunter forgives Miss Martian, M'gann, for lying to him about her true race, and Supergirl discovers Guardian's secret identity.

Episode 11: "The Martian Chronicles"

When M'gann's former White Martian mate, Armek, demands her surrender, J'onn takes her into DEO custody for protection. However, he soon realizes that he is actually housing Armek in disguise, who then hides by impersonating Winn. The Martian Manhunter and Miss Martian finally discover Armek, who dies in the struggle. However, Miss Martian opts to return to Mars anyway, to stand up to the corrupt members of the White Martian race.

Episode 12: "Luthors"

Lillian Luthor sees her day in court, but it's interrupted when Metallo's testimony turns into a violent attack with artificial kryptonite on the courtroom. It's soon publicized that Lena slipped Metallo the contraband kryptonite in her jail cell, but Supergirl doesn't believe Lena guilty of the crime. Lillian is freed in the ruckus and soon abducts her daughter, using Lena to gain access to one of Lex Luthor's weapon stockpiles. Supergirl arrives and confronts Lillian, managing to save Lena when Metallo's unstable artificial kryptonite explodes. Lillian and Cyborg Superman escape, and Lena is soon exonerated of any crime. In their personal life, Mon-El and Supergirl begin a romantic relationship, one immediately interrupted by the 5th-dimensional imp Mr. Mxyzptlk, who declares his own love for Supergirl.

Episode 13: "Mr. & Mrs. Mxyzptlk"

While Alex Danvers and Maggie Sawyer celebrate their budding relationship and their first Valentine's Day together, and Winn begins dating an alien named Lyra Strayd, the romantic holiday doesn't go so well for Kara. The villainous and powerful Mr. Mxyzptlk proposes to Supergirl and begins to create trouble for her until she finally agrees to marry him. At the Fortress of Solitude, Supergirl tricks Mxyzptlk into spelling out his own name backward, the only way to send the powerful imp back to his own dimension. With Mxy out of the way, Mon-El and Supergirl are finally free to pursue their own romantic relationship.

Episode 14: "Homecoming"

A suspicious alarm is triggered at the DEO, resulting in the recovering of Jeremiah Danvers. Jeremiah persuades J'onn to allow him back on the DEO staff, and he begins to dig into their files, eventually betraying his friends and family by downloading a list of known aliens to hand over to Cadmus. Now cybernetically enhanced, Jeremiah escapes the resulting confrontation when Alex refuses to shoot him.

Episode 15: "Exodus"

When Cadmus begins abducting aliens, Kara attempts to publish an article on the subject but is unable to produce a source due to her double identity. She decides to start a blog and share the information there. Kara's career issues don't stop Maggie and Alex from pursuing the investigation, even though Alex is temporarily suspended from the DEO for her blind spot in favor of her father, Jeremiah. When Alex is subsequently captured, Jeremiah reveals that Cadmus is going to deport their captured aliens off-world. Alex talks Jeremiah onto her side, and they successfully stop the deportation with the help of Supergirl. For her valiant efforts, Alex is reinstated to her job, even while back at CatCo, Kara is fired from her own due to her blog being a conflict of interest.

Episode 16: "Star-Crossed"

A large Daxamite spaceship arrives near Earth,
demanding Mon-El's return. The ship is commanded
by the king and queen of Daxam, Lar Gand and
Rhea, who just happen to be Mon-El's parents. After
accompanying Mon-El to the ship, Supergirl realizes
that Mon-El is a prince and has been blurring his past
from her intentionally, causing her to break up with him.
Meanwhile, Winn's girlfriend, Lyra, uses him as cover to
steal a painting to pay the debt of her brother, Bastian.
But when Winn, Guardian, and the DEO take down
Mandrax, the alien holding Bastian's debt, Winn and
Lyra reconcile. Back at the DEO, Supergirl encounters
the Music Meister, who puts her in a coma, where she
shares a dream reality with the Flash from Earth-1. In
The Flash, Season 3, Episode 17, Supergirl and Flash
must fight their way through a musical production to
return to the real world. Out of her coma, Supergirl
forgives Mon-El for keeping secrets from her.

Episode 17: "Distant Sun"

Unhappy with her son's relationship with a Kryptonian,
Rhea puts out a bounty on Supergirl's head, causing
several alien bounty hunters to attempt to cash in.
When Supergirl tries to talk some sense into Rhea, the
Daxamite queen attempts to kill her with kryptonite,
causing Mon-El to agree to stay with his parents if they
spare Supergirl's life. Supergirl and Martian Manhunter
try to rescue Mon-El, but in the end, Lar Gand decides
to let his son remain on Earth. Seeing this declaration
as a betrayal, Rhea murders her husband.

Episode 18: "Ace Reporter"

Now fast friends, Lena Luthor invites Kara to meet
her ex-boyfriend, Jack Spheer, a tech entrepreneur
about to release new nanotech to the world. Kara
suspects Jack's corruption and Mon-El steals a key
card to his office. However, they soon learn that Jack
is being controlled by his CFO Beth Breen, using his
nanotechnology against him. To save Supergirl from
an out-of-control Jack, Lena deactivates his nanobots,
killing him. It's a tragic story, but Kara is able to bring
one positive out of the mess: securing her old reporter
job again when she brings the story to Snapper Carr.
Meanwhile, the Guardian gains a new partner in the
field when Winn brings Lyra into the crime-fighting fold.

Episode 19: "Alex"

Rick Malverne, a former classmate of Alex's and Kara's from Midvale, kidnaps Alex in a bid to free his father, Peter Thompson, from prison. While Malverne knows her secret identity, Supergirl successfully holds Malverne in custody but is unable to learn the location of his sister, who will die without her intervention. Maggie attempts to break Thompson out of jail, but Supergirl intervenes, eventually talking Thompson into giving up a possible location for Alex. Supergirl finds her in the nick of time, saving Alex before the Martian Manhunter wipes Malverne's memories so that he forgets Supergirl's alter ego. Meanwhile, Rhea begins to work with the unsuspecting Lena Luthor, having Lena create a matter transporting device of her own design.

Episode 20: "City of Lost Children"

When Guardian helps a scared alien boy named Marcus, the child's telekinetic powers go haywire when Rhea activates her matter transporter. The same thing happens again when the boy leads Guardian back to a larger group of his alien people, the Phorians, but Guardian successfully calms them by calming Marcus first. With the device active, Mon-El confronts his mother, discovering she's transporting an entire fleet of Daxamite ships nearby, ready to conquer Earth. She then beams Mon-El and Lena Luthor with her to her ship.

Episode 21: "Resist"

The Daxamites invade National City while Rhea instructs Mon-El to marry Lena Luthor so they can serve as figureheads uniting the two planets. President Marsdin, alongside her friend Cat Grant, try to force the Daxamites to leave Earth, but Marsdin's plane, Air Force One, is shot down instead. Supergirl saves Cat as she and her former employer discover that Marsdin is an alien herself. They regroup with their allies at the alien dive bar in National City before Supergirl forms an uneasy alliance with Lillian Luthor and Cyborg Superman to use the Phantom Zone Projector to beam onboard the Daxamites' head ship. While Lillian and Cyborg Superman try to double-cross Supergirl, Supergirl anticipates their treachery and soon goes to face Rhea herself, intercepted by a mind-altered Superman.

Episode 22: "Nevertheless, She Persisted"

Under the influence of silver kryptonite, Superman attacks Supergirl, believing her to be his enemy, General Zod. Supergirl overpowers her cousin before challenging Rhea to the Daxamite rite of Dakkam Ur, a personal battle between two people to determine the outcome of an entire war. Rhea accepts, but when the two begin to fight, she refuses to end the invasion, no matter the outcome. Meanwhile, Lillian and Lena Luthor augment a Luthor device to disperse trace amounts of lead—the one weakness to the Daxamite people—into the air. Miss Martian even joins the fray with other heroic White Martians and fights alongside the Martian Manhunter. But ultimately, Supergirl activates the device as Rhea dies in the process. Supergirl is forced to place Mon-El in a rocket ship and send him away from Earth to spare his life. While Kara mourns his departure, she's unaware that he is sucked into a mysterious wormhole in space. As the smoke clears, Cat takes up her old job at CatCo and Alex proposes to Maggie. A new era is dawning for National City, but no one is aware of the enigmatic threat coming their way: a rocket ship sent from Krypton had landed on earth decades ago, bearing another infant, one destined to "reign."

Season 3

Episode 1: "Girl of Steel"

While Supergirl throws herself into crime-fighting, mourning the loss of Mon-El, Lena Luthor and James Olsen come into conflict with a power-hungry CEO named Morgan Edge. At CatCo, Kara quits her job and Snapper Carr is on sabbatical, while James Olsen is once again in charge due to the fact that Cat Grant has taken a job as the president's press secretary. As it turns out, Kara's role as Supergirl certainly begins to monopolize her time when Edge hires an assassin named Bloodsport to attack via submarine the ceremony debuting the new Supergirl statue. Supergirl stops Bloodsport, and Lena Luthor decides to buy CatCo to prevent Edge from purchasing the company. Lena talks Kara into taking her old job back, as Samantha Arias, a civilian who witnessed the statue attack, begins to suffer disturbing dreams.

Episode 2: "Triggers"

A bank robber named Psi goes on a crime spree in National City, using her powers to force Supergirl to experience her worst fears when the Girl of Steel attempts to stop her. Armed with a psychic inhibitor designed by Winn, Supergirl triumphs over her insecurities and captures the criminal. Meanwhile, Samantha Arias's daughter, Ruby, suspects her mother has superhuman abilities and puts herself in harm's way to test them. Luckily, Supergirl saves the day, as Samantha shows no signs of superhuman powers. Despite the chaos in her personal life, Samantha is soon offered Lena Luthor's position at L-Corp, as Lena has her hands full personally watching over CatCo.

Episode 3: "Far From The Tree"

After receiving a message from Miss Martian, the Martian Manhunter heads to Mars in his car-like spaceship alongside Supergirl. They uncover the benevolent White Martian resistance, and J'onn is soon reunited with his father, M'yrnn, though both believed the other to have been killed. While it takes some time to convince his father otherwise, J'onn succeeds in helping the resistance and returns to Earth with his father. Back on Earth, Maggie and Alex have a bridal shower, but a conflict arises when Maggie's father wants nothing to do with her life, and Alex agonizes over the fact that she wants children but Maggie does not.

Episode 4: "The Faithful"

A man named Thomas Coville is revealed to have been on the flight Supergirl saved when she first began her superheroic career in National City. Believing the Girl of Steel to be a sort of god-like figure, Thomas researched Krypton and not only discovered Kara's double life but found a Kryptonian bomb that he soon sets to detonate under a sporting arena to prove Supergirl's powers. The head of a cult that worships the sun god Rao, Coville is eventually stopped when Supergirl is proven fallible in his eyes when weakened by the kryptonite inside the bomb. Alex Danvers convinces Coville to help her shove the bomb down a large hole. In the end, Coville's adoration of Rao never wavers.

Episode 5: "Damage"

When several innocent National City children come down with lead poisoning, Morgan Edge throws public suspicion on Lena Luthor and her machine that dispersed minute traces of lead into the air to ward off the Daxamites. After a little investigation, Kara and Sam discover that Edge's chemical company poisoned a local public pool to sully Lena's reputation. Lena takes the slight personally and goes to murder Edge but is knocked unconscious. She awakes on a plane loaded with the same deadly chemical that Edge plans to use to taint the water supply, further implicating Lena. Supergirl rescues Lena and prevents the plane from crashing into the water supply. Meanwhile, Alex and Maggie realize they can't work past their differences when it comes to children and decide to break up.

Episode 6: "Midvale"

In an effort to get over both of their recent breakups, Alex and Kara head to their childhood home in Midvale. Through a flashback sequence, Kara remembers one of her first cases, an investigation into the death of her friend Kenny Li. While the local sheriff was revealed to be the culprit, Kara also met an FBI agent named Noel Neill, who was really the Martian Manhunter in disguise. Back in the present day, Kara and Alex grow stronger as sisters, ending a string of recent bickering.

Episode 7: "Wake Up"

While investigating a crashed spaceship buried underneath National City, Supergirl, Martian Manhunter, and Winn are shocked to find Mon-El in the inert craft, alongside several other people in stasis. Mon-El offers no real explanation, but instead attempts to escape the DEO, and eventually convinces Winn to accompany him back to his spaceship. Now cured of his lead poisoning, Mon-El reveals that he had entered a wormhole and has been living in the 31st century for seven years. In that time, he married Imra, a woman Supergirl had rescued from a malfunctioning stasis pod. Meanwhile, J'onn moves in with his father and Sam discovers the Kryptonian spaceship at her adoptive mother's house, an event that leads her to discover the Fortress of Sanctuary and learn she is destined to become a World Killer.

Episode 8: "Crisis on Earth-X, Part 1"

When the Flash sets out to marry his longtime love interest, Iris West, on Earth-1, the ceremony is crashed by Nazis from Earth-X, including Supergirl's own doppelgänger, Overgirl. Attending the festivities from Earth-38, Supergirl and Alex are drawn into a battle that continues into *Arrow*, Season 6, Episode 8; *The Flash*, Season 4, Episode 8; and *Legends of Tomorrow*, Season 3, Episode 8. Supergirl and her allies soon discover that Overgirl needs a heart transplant. When she is unable to obtain Supergirl's she dies, despite the best efforts of her husband, Green Arrow's Nazi doppelgänger. While Earth-1's Flash finally succeeds in marrying Iris when the smoke clears, and Green Arrow also marries his longtime love, Felicity Smoak, Alex has a brief fling of her own with the Legends team member known as White Canary.

Episode 9: "Reign"

With no memory of her time in the Fortress of Sanctuary, Sam tries to go back to her normal life just as odd Kryptonian symbols begin to appear all over National City. Meanwhile, Supergirl learns of Mon-El and Imra's future superhero team called the Legion and hosts a holiday party that she has to abruptly leave to investigate Reign, Sam's powerful masked alter ego. Later, Reign defeats Supergirl and drops the injured hero off a building. Back at CatCo, James Olsen and Lena Luthor begin a romantic relationship amid the chaos.

Episode 10: "Legion of Superheroes"

While trapped in her own mind in a coma, Kara is visited by the mind of Brainiac 5, another member of the Legion. Brainiac helps Kara work through her issues so she can escape into the real world. Meanwhile, Sam's Reign personality continues to usurp her body from time to time, though Sam remains mostly ignorant of her double life. She attacks Albatross Bay prison, where she is eventually forced to retreat thanks to the combined efforts of Supergirl and the Legion. Back at her Fortress of Sanctuary, Thomas Coville joins Reign's crusade.

Episode 11: "Fort Rozz"

Looking for more information on Reign, Supergirl gathers an all-female team to journey to Fort Rozz, since the prison is near a blue star, one which emits radiation deadly to males. With reluctant companions Livewire, Psi, and the not-so-reluctant Imra, Supergirl finds the object of her search, Priestess Rozz, but is ambushed by Reign. Livewire sacrifices herself so that Supergirl might live, and Psi forces Reign to retreat. With the new knowledge of two additional unaccounted-for World Killers, Supergirl and her allies return to Earth. But none witness a woman named Julia Freeman when she is hit by a car, revealing that she is in fact one of the World Killers Supergirl is searching for.

Episode 12: "For Good"

After Lena Luthor is nearly poisoned by an assassin, she and Kara secure invitations to a party Morgan Edge is throwing. Wanting revenge against Edge, Lena's mother, Lillian Luthor, sends a drone to kill Edge, who admits to the murder attempt in the hopes that Lena will save his life. Lillian then crashes the party wearing a Lex Corp warsuit, but Winn hacks the attack drone, sending it after Lillian instead. While Edge does his best to escape the situation, the Guardian prevents his escape and Lena leaves the scene with recorded evidence of Edge's confession.

Episode 13: "Both Sides Now"

The DEO invades Julia Freeman's home, and while she seems unaware of her status as a World Killer called Purity, she uses her powers against Supergirl and her allies, prompting her capture. With a seeming double personality, Purity escapes custody. Just when it appears that Supergirl managed to talk some sense into the World Killer, Reign arrives and takes Purity with her back to the Fortress of Sanctuary. Meanwhile, as Mon-El repairs his spacecraft with the help of the Martian Manhunter, he admits to feeling conflicted feelings for Supergirl, and he reveals that his relationship with Imra was an arranged marriage but one that involved real feelings after the fact. Imra soon presents Mon-El with her own confession: she and Brainiac 5 have a secret agenda while in this time period.

Episode 14: "Schott Through the Heart"

Kara's friends try for a fun karaoke night, but learn of the death of Toyman. Winn is soon reunited with his estranged mother, Mary. When Toyman's former security guard attempts to murder the rest of the Schott family, fulfilling the Toyman's last wishes, Winn stops this would-be killer with the help of Supergirl and Mon-El. Mon-El tells Supergirl that Saturn Girl and Brainiac 5 are really visiting this time period to stop Pestilence, who is destined to become the villain Blight in the future. Meanwhile, J'onn's father shows signs of dementia, and Lena Luthor is revealed to have Reign in her custody at L-Corp.

Episode 15: "In Search of Lost Time"

M'yrnn's mental deterioration becomes a danger to others when his unmonitored psychic abilities cause many of the DEO's employees to give into their inner rage. Reluctantly, he allows J'onn to place a power-dampening bracelet on him to curb his mind's effects on others. Meanwhile, Supergirl learns how to manipulate her cape during battle thanks to Mon-El's training, and Sam comes to terms with the fact that she is indeed Reign.

Episode 16: "Of Two Minds"

The third World Killer, Pestilence, rears her head in National City, and even manages to infect Winn and Alex with a deadly virus before Brainiac 5 develops a cure to the disease. Teaming with Purity, Pestilence manages to free Reign from Lena's custody and escapes, despite being confronted by Supergirl, Mon-El, and the Martian Manhunter.

Episode 17: "Trinity"

Brainiac 5 uses Legion technology to transport Supergirl's consciousness to the otherworldly dimension of the Valley of Juru where Samantha Arias is being held prisoner by Reign alongside Lena and Alex. They learn the location of the Fortress of Sanctuary, and then attack it in the real world. During their raid, Purity sees the error of her ways and kills Pestilence at the cost of her own life, destroying the Fortress in the process. When the smoke clears, Reign has escaped. Meanwhile, James reveals his Guardian identity to Lena, and Lena reveals that she had found a way to create kryptonite.

Episode 18: "Shelter from the Storm"

Fixated on killing Ruby and now possessing the powers of the fallen Purity and Pestilence, Reign journeys to the home of Sam's mother, Patricia Arias, and kills her, despite Supergirl's intervention. With the threat of Pestilence ended, the Legion returns to the future, except for Mon-El, who chooses to help Supergirl defeat Reign by staying behind. He soon battles Reign alongside Supergirl and Alex when the villain tracks down Ruby at a hidden Lex Luthor mansion. Reign is defeated and put back in Lena Luthor's custody, although not before Ruby learns the truth of her mother's double life.

Episode 19: "The Fanatical"

When members of Coville's cult try to build their own World Killer out of member Olivia, Supergirl talks some sense into the young girl. With the help of Mon-El, Supergirl separates Olivia from the Black-rock of Harun-El, a powerful and mysterious element. This returns Olivia to normal. Meanwhile, Reign grows stronger, threatening to escape Lena's captivity.

Episode 20: "Dark Side of the Moon"

While Alex defends herself from a revenge-seeking alien, Supergirl and Mon-El travel into outer space and discover not just the Blackrock, but Argo City, an entire Kryptonian metropolis spared from destruction. There Supergirl is reunited with her mother, Alura. She soon pleads Earth's case to Argo City's High Council, and is rewarded with a small sample of Blackrock, the very substance keeping Argo's citizens alive. Supergirl and Mon-El return to Earth just in time to confront an escaped Reign.

Episode 21: "Not Kansas"

While Supergirl and Mon-El battle Reign, Lena uses the time to make the Blackrock into a liquid formula. When Reign is injected with the solution, her dark side is seemingly destroyed, restoring Sam to her original personality. With the danger presumably at its end, Supergirl returns to Argo City with Mon-El, after saying her goodbyes on Earth. There, an attempt on her life by a cult member leads Kara to discover that Selena from Krypton's High Council is actually leading the Reign movement. But before Supergirl can stop her, Selena strands Kara on Argo City by stealing her spaceship, and journeys to Earth with two fellow witches.

Episode 22: "Make it Reign"

Selena and the other dark Kryptonian witches secure the blood of Purity and Pestilence in order to resurrect the inert Reign into her own separate form. Supergirl, Mon-El, and Alura find a way to travel to Earth with Winn's help. Meanwhile, J'onn begins to say goodbye to his dying father by using a Martian memory sharing ritual until the ceremony is interrupted when Reign begins to terraform the Earth into a New Krypton.

Episode 23 "Battles Lost and Won"

M'yrnn gives his life in order to merge with the planet and stop Reign's terraforming. Sam travels to Juru to drink from the source of Reign's powers, the legendary Fountain of Lilith. Later, she confronts Reign in the real world, only to have their fight taken back to Juru where she successfully bests her darker half with Supergirl's help. With the threat over, Alura returns to Krypton, Brainiac 5 joins the DEO, and Mon-El and Winn travel to the future. As if the world around her wasn't changing enough, Supergirl is even more surprised when J'onn steps down as DEO Director and awards the position to Alex, and James outs himself publicly as the Guardian. Kara prepares for her life's new chapter even as a strange duplicate of herself wanders the wastelands of Siberia, hinting of new dangers to come.

Cataloging-in-Publication Data has been applied for and can be obtained from the Library of Congress.

ISBN 978-1-4197-3170-9

Text by Matthew K. Manning
Cover design by Eddee Helms
Interior Design by Megan Sugiyama

Supergirl based on characters created by Jerry Siegel and Joe Schuster. By special arrangement with the Jerry Siegel family.

Printed and bound in U.S.A.
10 9 8 7 6 5 4 3 2 1

Amulet Books are available at special discounts when purchased in quantity for premiums and promotions as well as fundraising or educational use. Special editions can also be created to specification. For details, contact specialsales@abramsbooks.com or the address below.

Amulet Books® is a registered trademark of Harry N. Abrams, Inc.

ABRAMS The Art of Books
195 Broadway, New York, NY 10007
abramsbooks.com